To:
Cindy & Tony

From:
Grandma Williams

My favorite recipes are:

Healthy Entertaining
Here's To Your Health!

by Sue E. Willett, Home Economist

G&R PUBLISHING COMPANY
507 Industrial Street
Waverly, IA 50677

Printed in the United States of America
ISBN   1-56383-004-3

Published by G & R Publishing Co.,
Waverly, IA 50677

● ● ● ● ● ● ● ● ● ● ● ● ● ● ● ●

About the Author

Sue Willett graduated with honors from Central State University, Edmond Oklahoma, with a B.S. in Home Economics and a concentration in Business. Since 1985 she has proven her business talents as President of the M.S. Willett Co., Inc.; a leading edge company in product research, design, development and marketing.

In addition to the Health Series, Sue is author or co-author of four books and guides to healthy cooking and eating. After experiencing heart disease in her own family, Sue set about working to help others reduce their risks. Her books bring together lowfat - low cholesterol cooking with today's lifestyles. Ranging from traditional country cuisine to modern microwave dishes these recipes and tips provide for great tasting nutrition.

Sue and her family live in Cedar Falls, Iowa. Her husband and two children have been extremly helpful with taste-testing these recipes.

HEALTH SERIES

Fabulous Fiber Favorites
Subtitle: High Fiber Naturally

Kids Eat Healthy
Subtitle: Delicious and Nutritious

On A Healthy Wok
Subtitle: Quick and Easy

Microwave Cooking
Subtitle: Low Cholesterol and Lowfat

Healthy Entertaining
Subtitle: Here's To Your Health!

Heart Healthy Favorites
Subtitle: Low Cholesterol Cooking

Unibook Series

1100	Cookies	2300	Holiday Collection
1200	Casseroles	2400	Salads & Dressings
1300	Meat Dishes	2500	Wild Game
1400	Microwave	2600	Soups
1500	Cooking for "2"	3100	Fish & Seafood
1600	Slow Cooking	3200	Poultry
1700	Low Calorie	3300	My Own Recipes
1800	Canning & Freezing	3400	Low Cholesterol
1900	Pastries & Pies	3500	Chocoholic
2000	Charcoal Grilling	3600	Wine & Spirits
2100	Hors D'oeuvres	3700	Cajun
2200	Beef	3800	Household Hints

Ethnic Series

6100	Chinese
6200	Danish
6300	French
6400	German
6500	Greek
6600	Hungarian
6700	Italian
6800	Irish
6900	Japanese
7000	Mexican
7100	Norwegian
7200	Swedish

HEALTHY ENTERTAINING

Entertaining can be imaginative, exciting and a healthy experience. Sometimes when we think of having people over for dinner, we think that we have to cook up our most exclusive, rich recipes, which are often very high in fat, cholesterol, salt and calories. This does not, however, have to be the case. In fact, in this new age of health conscious consumers, we can cook up a very healthy dinner party that tastes great and we will make a very warm, memorable experience for our guests. It shows that you genuinly care about your guest's health and well-being.

Here is a handy cookbook for you to pull out and use for your next healthy celebration. It includes special ideas on how to incorporate a healthy menu plan into your next brunch, birthday party, picnic or dinner party. You will be amazed at the great tasting results and the sparkling new fun ideas that you can adapt to your household, your friends and your celebrations. Home is truly where the heart is, and you can keep your heart and body healthier, even during special occasions.

HERE'S TO YOUR HEALTH!

TIPS FOR A HEALTHY PARTY MENU

1. For a non-alcoholic party beverage, try a healthy spritz of sparkling water and fruit juice blended with ice.

2. For appetizers offer lowfat dips, lowfat cheese, whole grain crackers, fresh vegetables and assorted fresh fruits.

3. Select and serve lowfat and fat-free foods. Some examples include whole grains, fresh fruits and vegetables and legumes.

4. Prepare broiled or poached items instead of fried or batter dipped foods.

5. Limit saturated fats, such as fatty meats, lard and butter. Select small amounts of polyunsaturated fats. Select from corn, sunflower, safflower, cottonseed, soybean, sesame or olive oils.   II

6. Avoid serving foods that are creamed, in a gravy, sauteed, fried, in a butter sauce or buttered.

7. Avoid preparing casseroles that are escalloped, made au gratin or covered in cheese sauce.

8. Purchase meats, fish or poultry that do not have a lot of visible fat. Trim off all visible skin and fat in meal preparation.

9. Broil, bake, steam or poach meats. The more simply-prepared, the better it will be for a healthier main coarse.

10. Make a simple, light, low sugar dessert. Fresh fruits work well for dessert.

DRESSING UP YOUR TABLE:

You can help create the mood of the party by the table setting. You can use your fine china for elegant entertaining, or your starter set of pottery for an informal relaxed atmosphere, decorated with earthenware serving dishes and colorful napkins and bread baskets. You may even want to mix and match your pieces of formal and informal dinner service, and that is OK too.

Flatware can be plain or fancy these days. There is a broad choice range and there is no law about it. Afterall, who wants to polish silver every time you entertain.

Glassware should be clear and in traditional shapes for a formal dinner, but for an informal dinner almost anything goes. Informal dinner glasses can add alot of color if you like, and interesting shapes can be used.

Your choice of table linens depends on the feeling that you are trying to

● ● ● ● ● ● ● ● ● ● ● ● ● ● ●

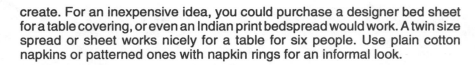

create. For an inexpensive idea, you could purchase a designer bed sheet for a table covering, or even an Indian print bedspread would work. A twin size spread or sheet works nicely for a table for six people. Use plain cotton napkins or patterned ones with napkin rings for an informal look.

For the table decoration, remember not to have such a large one that it cuts off communication across the table. For healthy entertaining, use a pretty bowl of fresh fruit that can later be used for dessert with lowfat cheeses for your centerpiece. An arrangement of fresh vegetables, shiny eggplant, artichoke and violet turnips set in a long narrow basket on a bed of green leaves would be very nice. These two ideas would carry out your fresh and healthy party theme. Proper lighting and candles can also be a nice enhancement for the general ambience of your party. A little ingenuity and creativity can help you work with materials that you already have on hand. Your dinner party will be an appreciated success! Your party can look good, taste good and be good for you too!!!
Enjoy some healthy entertaining!

HEALTHY SUBSTITUTIONS

INGREDIENT:	SUBSTITUTION:
EGGS	You can use 2 teaspoons polyunsaturated oil and 1 egg white. There are cholesterol-free egg substitutes also available commercially. Check label.
MILK	Skim milk or non-fat dry milk.
BUTTER	Polyunsatured margarine or oil.
SOUR CREAM	Use lowfat yogurt. May also use blended cottage cheese and may mix it with lowfat

yogurt. May mix ½ cup lowfat cottage cheese, ½ tablespoon lemon juice and 1 tablespoon skim milk.

WHIPPED CREAM

¼ cup non-fat dry milk with 1½ tablespoons sugar, 1½ tablespoons oil, ½ teaspoon gelatin, 1 teaspoon cold water, 1½ tablespoons boiling water and ¼ cup ice water.

First mix gelatin with cold water. Stir and add boiling water until dissolves. Beat non-fat dry milk and ice water in cold bowl on high until peaks. Still beating add sugar, oil and gelatin. Place in refrigerator until ready.

CREAM CHEESE	Blend ½ cup dry lowfat cottage cheese and 2 tablespoons margarine. You may add a small amount of skim milk in blending.
BUTTERMILK	2 cups buttermilk = 2 cups lukewarm non-fat milk and 2 tablespoons lemon juice. Beat mixture briskly.
HOLLANDAISE SAUCE	Slowly beat 4 tablespoons hot water with 1 cup low cal mayonnaise. Stir until heated through. Add 2 tablespoons lemon juice. Pour over favorite vegetables
SALT	Combine 1 tablespoon paprika, 1 tablespoon garlic powder, 1 tablespoon onion powder, 1 tablespoon dry mustard, ½ tablespoon white pepper, ½ teaspoon ground thyme and 1 teaspoon crushed basil leaves.

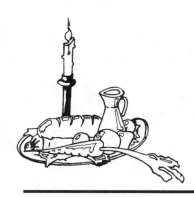

MENU IDEAS

HEALTHY PARTY MENU IDEAS

BRUNCH MENU:

Gourmet Omelet
Mushroom Quiches
Easy Crepes
Marinated Fresh Fruit Bowl
Date Coffee Cake
Blueberry Raisin Bran Muffins
Mushroom, Spinach and Cheese
  Squares
Juice of your choice, Coffee or Tea

1

GOURMET OMELET

2 tsp. chopped onion
¼ C. sliced mushrooms
1 tsp. broth or water
1 tsp. minced chives
2 tsp. chopped parsley
2 tsp. diced green chilies
2 T. crabmeat
Fresh parsley for garnish

2 T. lowfat Cheddar cheese, grated
2 T. chopped tomato
¼ to ½ C. egg substitute per
  person
1 T. water per person
Dash salt
Dash pepper
1 to 2 slices tomato per person
for garnish

Saute onion, mushrooms and green chilies until tender in small amount of, broth or water. Beat eggs, water, salt and pepper with a fork until mixture is blended. Heat an 8" Teflon skillet over medium heat until a drop of water sizzles when sprinkled on the pan. Pour in eggs. Tilt pan to spread evenly throughout and at an even depth. Using a fork, stir rapidly through top of

2

uncooked eggs. Shake pan frequently to keep eggs moving. When egg is set, remove pan from heat. Spoon desired fillings across center. Flip sides of omelet over, envelope style, to hold in filling. Tilt pan and roll omelet over onto plate. Garnish with tomatoes and parsley.

MUSHROOM QUICHES

½ C. egg substitute or
  egg substitute with cheese
1 T. sliced scallions
1 T. snipped fresh dill or 1 tsp.
  dried dill weed

½ tsp. dry mustard
Dash ground black pepper
30 lg. mushroom caps

In medium bowl, stir together egg substitute, scallions, dill, mustard and pepper. Arrange mushroom caps on 15½x10½x1" baking pan. Spoon egg mixture into caps. Bake at 375° for 10 to 15 minutes or until set. Serve immediately.

FOR MICROWAVE: Prepare mushrooms as above. Arrange 10 stuffed mushrooms in a 9" microwave-proof pie plate. Microwave on high (100%) power for 2 to 2½ minutes, rotating dish ½ turn after 1 minute. Repeat with remaining mushrooms.

EASY CREPES

½ C. egg substitute
½ C. skim milk
½ C. cold water
1 C. flour

2 T. safflower oil
½ tsp. sugar
⅛ tsp. salt

Beat egg substitute, milk and water lightly. Add remaining ingredients; blend. Pour enough batter into a preheated 5" Teflon crepe pan to coat bottom of pan; tilt pan to spread batter. Cook for 1 minute or just until set. Turn and cook for 1 minute longer or until browned. Great with fresh strawberries and special whipped cream.

MARINATED FRESH FRUIT BOWL

FRUIT MARINADE:
½ C. honey
¼ C. water
¼ C. lime juice
¼ C. orange-flavored
  liqueur or orange juice

FRUIT:
1 C. honeydew melon balls or cubes
1 C. watermelon balls or cubes
2 lg. nectarines or peaches, peeled,
  sliced
½ C. strawberries, halved, if desired

In small saucepan, combine honey and water. Bring to a boil. Reduce heat; simmer 5 minutes. Stir in lime juice and orange liqueur. Cool completely. In medium bowl, combine fruit. Pour marinade over fruit; mix gently. Cover; refrigerate 1 to 2 hours to blend flavors. Serve 8 (½ cup each).

DATE COFFEE CAKE

CAKE:
⅓ C. mashed bananas, (mash ripe banana with a fork)
½ C. oil
¾ C. egg substitute
1 tsp. vanilla extract
1¼ C. water

1 C. unbleached white flour
2 C. oat bran
1 tsp. baking soda
2 tsp. baking powder
1½ C. chopped dates

TOPPING:
⅓ C. chopped dates
⅓ C. chopped walnuts

⅓ C. flaked coconut, optional

Beat together mashed banana and oil until creamy. Add egg substitute, vanilla extract and water; beat. Measure in flour, oat bran, baking soda and baking powder; beat well. Stir in 1½ cups chopped dates. Spoon batter into

8

an oiled and floured 9x13" baking pan. Spread batter evenly in pan. Combine topping ingredients and sprinkle over batter. Bake at 350° for 20 to 25 minutes or until a knife inserted comes out clean. Cool on wire rack. Serves 8 to 10.

BLUEBERRY RAISIN BRAN MUFFINS

½ C. margarine
1 C. sugar
½ C. egg substitute
2½ C. flour
2½ tsp. baking soda
2 C. buttermilk substitute
  (see substitution section)

1 C. 100% Bran
1 C. boiling water
2 C. All Bran
½ C. chopped nuts
½ C. raisins
½ C. blueberries

Cream margarine with sugar and egg substitute. Sift flour with baking soda and add to first mixture, alternating with buttermilk substitute; mix well. Combine 100% Bran and boiling water. Let stand for 1 minute. Add this to mixture and stir thoroughly. Then fold in All Bran, nuts, raisins, and blueberries. Makes 24 muffins. Bake at 400° for 15 minutes.

MUSHROOM, SPINACH AND CHEESE SQUARES

3 T. dry white wine
¾ lb. fresh mushrooms, cleaned and sliced
4 green onions, thinly sliced
1 tsp. low-sodium vegetable seasoning
1 T. Worcestershire sauce

3-10 oz. pkgs. frozen chopped spinach, defrosted and well drained
1½ C. soft whole wheat crumbs
1 pt. Weight Watchers cottage cheese, rinsed and drained
6 egg whites

Bring wine to a boil in a nonstick skillet. Add mushrooms and green onions and saute until just tender. Add vegetable seasoning, Worcestershire sauce and drained spinach. Blend well and transfer to a mixing bowl. Add bread crumbs and drained cottage cheese. Blend. Beat egg whites until stiff and fold into spinach mixture. Spray a 9x13x2" glass baking dish with nonstick spray and place spinach mixture in dish. Bake, uncovered, in a preheated 350° oven for 30 minutes, or until firm. Let stand 10 minutes before cutting into 8 portions for serving. 12

VARIATIONS: May be cut into smaller squares and served as an appetizer.
Frozen chopped broccoli maybe substituted for the spinach.

LUNCHEON MENU:

Fresh Strawberry Soup (appetizer)
Spinach Salad in Tomato Tulip Cups
Chicken with Fruit Toss
Great Bread Sticks
Cheesecake
Coffee or Tea

14

FRESH STRAWBERRY SOUP

2 pts. fresh sweet, ripe
  strawberries, washed, then
  hulled and cut in halves
1 T. cornstarch
1 C. fresh orange juice

1 C. red wine
¼ C. frozen unsweetened apple
  juice concentrate, or to taste
1 C. nonfat yogurt
Fresh mint leaves for garnish

Puree half of the strawberries in a blender or food processor. Add remaining berries and puree. Blend cornstarch with ¼ cup orange juice in a 2-quart saucepan. Add remaining orange juice, the red wine, apple juice concentrate and pureed strawberries. Heat just to boiling over medium heat, stirring frequently; remove from heat. Cool. Stir in nonfat yogurt with a whisk. Cover and refrigerate 2 to 4 hours before serving. This soup may be frozen. Serve in chilled glass or elegant china bowls garnished with whole or chopped fresh mint leaves and a stemmed whole strawberry.

SPINACH SALAD IN TOMATO TULIP CUPS

DRESSING:
2 T. tarragon vinegar
2 T. oil
½ to 1 tsp. dill weed
¼ tsp. salt
¼ tsp. garlic powder
¼ tsp. dry mustard
Dash pepper

SALAD:
1½ C. cooked rice
10 oz. pkg. frozen chopped spinach, thawed, squeezed to drain
1 C. chopped tomato
½ C. sliced green onions
½ C. sliced celery
6 lg. tomatoes
2 T. unsalted sunflower nuts

In small bowl, combine all dressing ingredients; blend well. In medium bowl, combine cooked rice, spinach, chopped tomato, green onions and celery; mix well. Pour dressing over salad; toss well. Refrigerate 1 hour to blend flavors. To prepare tomato tulips, hollow out stem portion at center of each tomato. Make 6 cuts from center of each tomato to outside, making sure not

16

to cut through bottom skin. Spoon about ⅔ cup salad mixture into each tomato tulip. Sprinkle with sunflower nuts. Serves 6.

CHICKEN WITH FRUIT TOSS

¼ C. water
¼ C. frozen tangerine juice
  concentrate
1 T. lemon juice or lime juice
1 tsp. cornstarch
2 sm. pineapples, chilled
2 C. shredded lettuce

1½ C. cubed cooked chicken
1 orange, peeled and sectioned
1 kiwi fruit, peeled, sliced and
  quartered
2 oz. Monterey Jack cheese, cut into
  1" long thin strips

For dressing: In a small saucepan, stir together the water, tangerine juice concentrate, lemon or lime juice and cornstarch. Cook and stir until thickened and bubbly. Cook and stir for 2 minutes more. Remove saucepan from heat. Cover surface with waxed paper or clear plastic wrap. Cool slightly without stirring; chill. Meanwhile, use a sharp knife to cut the pineapples lengthwise in half, crown and all. Remove hard cores from pineapples. Cut out pineapple meat, leaving shells intact. Set pineapple shells aside. Cut pineapple meat into bite-size chunks. Set aside 3 cups of the chunks. (Refrigerate remaining pineapple for another use.) In a medium mixing bowl combine the reserved pineapple chunks, lettuce, chicken, orange sections, kiwi fruit and cheese. Pour dressing over fruit mixture. Toss lightly to coat. Immediately spoon the fruit mixture into pineapple shells. Place shells on 4 salad plates. Makes 4 servings.

GREAT BREAD STICKS

2 pkgs. active dry yeast
⅔ C. warm water
2¾ C. water
2 T. safflower oil
3 tsp. salt
3⅓ C. whole wheat flour

4½ C. all-purpose flour
Tub safflower margarine
2 egg whites, with 1 T. water,
  beaten until frothy
Sesame seeds

Place yeast in ⅔ cup warm water. Heat remaining water, safflower oil and salt to lukewarm; pour into large mixing bowl. Add wheat flour and dissolved yeast. Mix until smooth. Gradually add all-purpose flour. Remove to lightly floured surface. Knead for 10 minutes or until smooth; form into ball. Place in medium bowl, greased with margarine. Cover and let rise in a warm place, about 2 hours. Punch down and cut dough into 5 dozen equal size pieces. Roll each between palms into 6" rope. Place 2" apart on a baking sheet. Cover and let rise in a warm place for 30 to 60 minutes. Brush with beaten

20

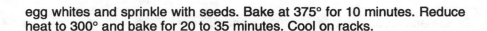

egg whites and sprinkle with seeds. Bake at 375° for 10 minutes. Reduce heat to 300° and bake for 20 to 35 minutes. Cool on racks.

CHEESECAKE

2 envs. unflavored gelatin
¼ C. sugar, divided
¼ tsp. salt
2 pkts. Butter Buds, divided
½ C. plus 3 T. unsweetened
 pineapple juice, divided
1 C. lowfat milk
½ C. egg substitute

1-8 oz. container dry-curd cottage
 cheese
½ C. juice packed crushed
 pineapple, drained
1 T. grated lemon peel
½ C. graham cracker crumbs
1 tsp. vanilla
1 T. lemon juice

Mix gelatin, 3 tablespoons sugar, salt, 1 packet Butter Buds, ½ cup pineapple juice, milk and ½ of egg substitute in top of double boiler. Place over boiling water and cook, stirring constantly, until gelatin dissolves and mixture thickens slightly. Cool. In medium-size bowl, beat cottage cheese until smooth. (Use a potato masher for best results.) Beat in crushed pineapple and lemon peel. Add cooled gelatin mixture. In separate small bowl, combine graham cracker crumbs, remaining packet of Butter Buds and vanilla. Add remaining pineapple juice and lemon juice. Mix well and stir into cheese mixture. In separate bowl, beat other half of egg substitute until firm. Gradually add remaining sugar and beat until stiff. Fold into cheese-crumb mixture. Pour into 9" pie plate. Chill until firm.

MEXICAN DINNER MENU:

Nachos (appetizers)
Salsa Dip
Burritos
Chicken Fajitas
Mexican Turkey Tortillas
Mexican Eggplant
Spanish Rice
Beverage of your choice

NACHOS

5-8" flour tortillas
2 med. tomatoes, peeled,
   seeded and chopped
1-4 oz. can diced green chili
   peppers, drained

½ tsp. chili powder
Several dashes bottled hot
   pepper sauce
1 C. shredded mozzarella cheese
   (4 oz.)

Stack tortillas and cut the whole stack into 8 wedges to make 40 wedges total. Spread evenly in a single layer on 2 medium baking sheets. Bake in a 375° oven for 10 to 15 minutes or until wedges are dry and crisp. Meanwhile, combine tomatoes, chili peppers, chili powder and hot pepper sauce. Spoon the tomato mixture over wedges and top with cheese. Broil 1 baking sheet at a time, 4 to 5" from heat, about 1½ minutes or until the cheese is melted. Slide onto a serving platter. Serve nachos at once. Makes 8 (5 nachos each) servings.

SALSA DIP

1-28 oz. can plum tomatoes
  in puree
1 sm. onion, red or white
½ green pepper
1-3½ oz. can green chilies
1 clove garlic
1½ T. red wine vinegar

1 tsp. oregano
½ tsp. cumin
½ tsp. Italian herb seasoning
½ C. cilantro
1 whole green pepper for serving,
  optional

Add all ingredients, except whole green pepper, to food processor or blender. Blend until well chopped. Don't overchop. (If salt-free tomatoes are used, the sodium content will be considerably lower.) Store in covered container in refrigerator. May be stored several weeks.

BURRITOS

4 corn tortillas
½ C. lowfat Cheddar cheese,
 grated

1 T. finely chopped tomato
2 T. chopped green chilies
1 T. finely chopped onion

Lay tortillas flat; sprinkle with cheese, green chilies, tomato and onion. Roll into a tight roll. Heat to 350° for 5 to 6 minutes. Serve with mashed avocado mixed with non-fat yogurt.

CHICKEN FAJITAS

2 whole chicken breasts, split,
  boned and skinned
1 lg. red onion, cut into rings
1 lg. sweet pepper, cut into
  thick slices

¾ C. mild taco sauce
¼ C. lime juice
4 warmed flour tortillas

Cut chicken into ½" thick slices. In a 10x6x2" microwave-safe baking dish, combine the chicken, onion, pepper, taco sauce and lime juice. Mix well. Cover the dish with plastic wrap and microwave on high (100% power) 5 minutes per pound of chicken breast. Turn one-half turn every 5 minutes until chicken is done. Chicken and vegetables will be tender. Divide chicken and vegetables among flour tortillas and wrap. Makes 4 servings.

MEXICAN TURKEY TORTILLAS

½ lb. ground turkey
1-10 oz. pkg. frozen corn
4 flour tortillas

3 T. taco sauce
¼ C. shredded lowfat Cheddar
  cheese
⅓ C. sliced ripe olives

In 1-quart microwave-safe casserole, crumble the turkey. Add frozen corn. Cover and microwave on high (100% power) for 8 to 10 minutes or until turkey is no longer pink. Stir once at 5 minutes. Place about ½ cup of turkey mixture in each flour tortilla. Roll up with filling inside. Place, seam side down, in 8" square microwave-safe baking dish. Cover with waxed paper and microwave on high for 2 to 3 minutes or until heated through. Top with taco sauce and sprinkle with cheese and olives. Makes 4 servings.

MEXICAN EGGPLANT

1 med. eggplant, peeled and
  cut into cubes
1-16 oz. can tomatoes or 4
  med. fresh tomatoes,
  peeled and chopped

1 garlic clove, minced
2 T. chopped onion
¼ tsp. chili powder
Dash of pepper

Combine all ingredients in skillet and simmer gently 15 to 20 minutes or until
eggplant is tender. Serves 6.

SPANISH RICE

1 med. onion, chopped	1 C. uncooked long-grain white
1 sm. green pepper, chopped	rice
1 clove garlic, minced	½ tsp. seasoned salt
1 T. vegetable or olive oil	⅛ tsp. pepper
1-16 oz. can tomatoes	¼ tsp. chili powder
	¼ tsp. cumin

In a 2-quart casserole, combine onion, green pepper, garlic and oil. Microwave, covered, on high for 2 to 3 minutes or until tender. Drain tomatoes, reserving liquid and chopping tomatoes. Add enough water to reserved liquid to make 2 cups. Add to onion mixture with tomatoes, rice and seasoning. Microwave covered, on high for 5 minutes or until boiling. Microwave on medium low (30% power) for 14 to 16 minutes or until rice is tender. Let stand, covered, 5 minutes. Serves 6.

ITALIAN DINNER MENU:

Low Meat Lasagna
Low Cal Creamy Pasta Alfredo
Italian Green Beans
Tasty French Bread
Beverage of your choice

LOW MEAT LASAGNA

1 C. ricotta cheese or lowfat
  cottage cheese
¼ C. egg substitute
½ C. grated Parmesan cheese
  or less

1 recipe Meat Sauce (below)
8 oz. lasagna, cooked for 7 minutes
  and drained
6 oz. mozzarella cheese, sliced

In bowl, stir together ricotta, egg substitute and ¼ cup of the Parmesan cheese. In 11x7x2" baking dish spread ½ cup of the Meat Sauce. Layer ⅓ of the lasagna noodles, 1¼ cups sauce, ½ of the ricotta mixture and ⅓ of the mozzarella cheese. Repeat once. Top with remaining noodles, sauce, mozzarella and Parmesan cheese. Bake at 350° for 30 minutes or until bubbly. Let stand for 15 minutes before serving. Makes 6 to 8 servings.

MEAT SAUCE:

1 T. corn oil
½ lb. ground beef
½ C. chopped onion
2 cloves garlic, minced
¼ C. chopped parsley
1-28 oz. can tomatoes

⅓ C. tomato paste
1 tsp. sugar
1 tsp. dried basil leaves
¼ tsp. salt
½ tsp. dried oregano leaves
⅛ tsp. pepper

Heat corn oil over medium heat. Add the next 4 ingredients. Cook, stirring for 10 minutes or until beef is browned. In blender container place tomatoes and cover. Blend on high speed for 30 seconds or until chopped. Add to beef mixture. Stir in remaining ingredients. Bring to boil. Reduce heat and simmer, stirring occasionally, 45 minutes. Makes 3¾ cups.

LOW CAL CREAMY PASTA ALFREDO

1½ C. 1% lowfat cottage cheese
2 cloves garlic, halved
½ C. skim milk
2 T. all-purpose flour
3 tsp. fresh lemon juice
1 tsp. leaf basil, crumbled

½ tsp. dry mustard
½ tsp. pepper
¼ tsp. salt
8 oz. rotelle pasta
1 med.-sized ripe tomato,
  halved, seeded and coarsely
  chopped

Place cottage cheese, garlic and skim milk in container of food processor or electric blender. Whirl, scraping down sides of bowl, until smooth (no lumps), 3 to 5 minutes. Add flour, lemon juice, basil, mustard, pepper and salt. Whirl to blend well. * Turn into a medium-sized saucepan; reserve. Cook rotelle according to package directions, drain. Turn into large bowl. Heat cream sauce over medium-low heat to thicken slightly. Stir often until sauce just begins to bubble, 1 to 2 minutes; do not allow to come to a full boil. Remove

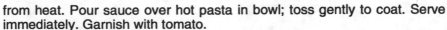

from heat. Pour sauce over hot pasta in bowl; toss gently to coat. Serve immediately. Garnish with tomato.

*NOTE: This sauce can be made several hours ahead and then refrigerated until ready to use.

ITALIAN GREEN BEANS

3 T. oil
½ C. chopped onion
1 clove garlic, minced
1-20 oz. can tomatoes,
  drained
¼ tsp. salt

¼ tsp. freshly ground black pepper
¼ tsp. oregano
1 bay leaf
2 lbs. green beans or 3 pkgs. frozen

Saute onions in saucepan with oil. Add the garlic, tomatoes, salt, pepper, oregano and bay leaf; bring to a boil and cook over low heat 20 minutes. Add the fresh or frozen beans to the tomato mixture. Cover and cook over low heat 30 minutes.

TASTY FRENCH BREAD

1 cake or pkg. yeast	¾ tsp. salt
1 C. lukewarm water	3½ sifted flour
½ tsp. sugar	

Soften the yeast in the water, mixed with the sugar and salt. Beat in 2 cups flour until very smooth. Add enough of the remaining flour to make a soft dough. Turn out onto a floured surface and knead until smooth and elastic. Place in an oiled bowl, cover, and let rise in a warm place until double in bulk, about 1 hour. Punch down and roll out into a rectangle, about 10x18". Roll up from the wide side like a jelly roll. Be sure to roll tightly. Pinch the edges together and place on a baking pan. Cut gashes 3" apart and about ⅛" deep. Brush top with cold water and let rise in a warm place 1½ hours. Bake in a preheated 400° oven for 40 minutes or until browned. Brush with cold water every 10 minutes for a crusty top. Makes 1-18" loaf of bread.

**MONGOLIAN FIRE POT
PARTY MENU:**
(Chinese Fondue)

Mongolian Fire Pot
Oriental Tea

MONGOLIAN FIREPOT

STOCK:
10 C. chicken broth
2 whole lean chicken breasts
1 med. onion, sliced
2 stalks celery, cut into ½" slices
2 T. dry sherry
1 tsp. sesame oil
1 piece fresh gingerroot,
  cut into thin slices

DIPPING SAUCES:
Sweet-sour sauce
Hot mustard mixed with water
¼ C. low salt soy sauce mixed
  with 2 tsp. sesame oil and ⅛ tsp.
  pepper
SEASON FOR CHICKEN:
½ tsp. salt
½ tsp. sugar

42

HOT POT:
1 whole lean chicken breast
¾ lb. prawns
½ lb. lean pork
8 green onions
½ head Chinese cabbage
1 can bamboo shoots
8 oz. bean curd (tofu)

SEASONING FOR PORK:
½ tsp. salt
½ tsp. sugar
¾ tsp. low salt soy sauce
Dash pepper
1 tsp. cornstarch

STOCK: Place all ingredients in stock pot. Cover and bring to boil. Reduce heat to low and simmer stock about 2 hours. Strain stock and place in hot pot or wok.

FIREPOT INGREDIENTS: Skin and bone chicken. Cut into thin 1½" strips. Place in small bowl, add chicken seasonings, mix and set aside. Shell, devein and wash prawns. Place in bowl and set aside. Slice pork into thin 1" strips. Place in small bowl, add pork seasonings, mix and set aside. Wash and cut onions into 2" pieces and set aside. Finely shred cabbage and set aside.

Drain bamboo shoots. Drain bean curd and cut into 1x¼" pieces. Arrange all ingredients on serving plates.

SERVING INSTRUCTIONS: Heat chicken broth in wok that has been placed in center of table. Arrange the serving dishes around the wok. Provide each guest with a small bowl, a pair of chopsticks, a 2" Chinese wire strainer and a small dish for dipping sauce. Each person selects the foods of his or her choice and places them in the strainer. The diner then immerses the strainer in the broth until the food is cooked. Thus, each person cooks the foods to suit his or her own taste.

Suggested cooking times: prawns, onions, cabbage, bamboo shoots and bean curd, about 1 minute; chicken and pork, about 2 minutes.

HALLOWEEN PARTY MENU:

Nutritious Carrot-Cheese Spread (appetizers)
Oat Bran Cracker Squares
Halloween Pumpkin Casserole
Pear and Red Grape Salad with Lemon Honey Dressing
Bran Dinner Rolls
Rice Crispie Halloween Treats

NUTRITIOUS CARROT-CHEESE SPREAD

¾ C. grated carrots
½ hard-boiled egg, grated
2½ T. salad dressing
1 tsp. grated onion

½ tsp. lemon juice
Dash of pepper
½ C. lowfat colby cheese, grated

In a small bowl, combine carrots, egg, onion, cheese, lemon juice, salad dressing and pepper. Mix well and refrigerate until serving time. Makes about ¾ cup spread.

SERVING SUGGESTIONS: Serve as a spread on pita bread or whole wheat bread for a sandwich. For a party, use a Teddy Bear cookie cutter to cut a bear out of the whole wheat bread. Spread with mixture as topping.

OAT BRAN CRACKER SQUARES

1½ C. oat bran
½ C. all-purpose flour
⅛ tsp. salt

Pinch baking soda
¼ C. margarine, softened
1½ tsp. honey
¼ C. hot water

Preheat oven to 325°. In a large bowl combine the oat bran, flour, salt and baking soda. Cut in margarine until mixture resembles coarse corn meal. Dissolve the honey in the hot water; blend into the oat bran mixture. Add more flour if dough is too wet for rolling. Divide dough in half. Roll each half to ⅛" thickness on a floured surface. Cut the dough into 2" squares. Place squares on a baking sheet sprayed lightly with vegetable oil cooking spray. Prick each squares 3 times with a fork. Bake at 325° for 18 to 22 minutes or until lightly browned. Cool on wire rack. Makes 50 to 55-2" crackers.

HALLOWEEN PUMPKIN CASSEROLE

1 sm. to med. pumpkin
1 lb. lean ground beef
1 lb. ground turkey
⅓ C. chopped onion
1-10 oz. can low-salt cream
  of chicken soup

½ C. low-salt soy sauce
2 T. brown sugar
¼ tsp. pepper
¼ tsp. seasoned salt, optional
2 C. cooked rice
1-4 oz. can sliced mushrooms,
  drained

Cut top off of pumpkin; clean out pumpkin saving the seeds for use in Toasted Pumpkin Seeds. In a skillet, cook the beef, turkey and onion until meat is no longer pink; drain. In a large bowl combine the chicken soup, soy sauce, brown sugar, pepper and seasoned salt; mix well. Add the meat mixture, mushrooms and cooked rice; stir until well combined. Spoon mixture into the hollowed-out pumpkin, placing lid back on. Place pumpkin on a foil-lined cookie sheet and bake at 375° for 1½ to 2 hours. Use as a centerpiece on

tables with leaves around the pumpkin. This is good served with baked apples.

PEAR AND RED GRAPE SALAD

3 C. torn spinach leaves
1 med. pear, sliced
1 C. seedless red grapes
½ C. sliced celery
¼ C. pecan pieces
½ C. Lemon Honey Dressing

Place spinach leaves on large platter. Arrange pear, grapes, celery and pecans decoratively on top. Drizzle with ½ of dressing. Serve with remaining dressing. Makes 4 servings.

LEMON HONEY DRESSING

¼ C. lemon juice   2 T. honey
2 T. special oil

In container with lid, combine all dressing ingredients. Shake well. Cover and refrigerate to blend flavors. Store in refrigerator. Makes ½ cup.

BRAN DINNER ROLLS

¾ C. oat-bran cereal
½ C. self-rising flour
¾ C. skim milk

2 T. honey
3 T. vegetable oil

Run the oat-bran cereal through a blender to mill the cereal to a flour like consistency. Blend in the self-rising flour. Blend in the other ingredients and drop the batter onto a cookie sheet sprayed with vegetable oil cooking spray. This will make about 12 rolls. Bake them at 375° for 8 to 10 minutes or until just barely browned.

RICE CRISPIE HALLOWEEN TREATS

40 regular size marshmallows
3 T. safflower oil
½ tsp. clear vanilla

4 drops orange food coloring
4 C. rice cereal
Raisins

Combine marshmallows and oil in a saucepan. Cook over medium heat until marshmallows are melted, stirring constantly. Add vanilla and food coloring, mix well. Add rice cereal mixing until well coated. Shape mixture into balls. Decorate with raisins to resemble face of a pumpkin. Mixture also can be dropped by teaspoonfuls onto a sheet of wax paper for cookies. Refrigerate.

THANKSGIVING MENU:

Savory Stuffed Mushrooms
  (appetizers)
Cornish Hens with Orange Stuffing
Harvest Beans
Apple Sweet Potato Scallop
Orange-Cranberry Salad
Bran-Cran Bread
Pumpkin-Yogurt Pie
Coffee or Tea

SAVORY STUFFED MUSHROOMS

1 lb. med, fresh mushrooms,
  (about 25 to 30)
3 T. margarine
¾ C. dry bread crumbs
½ C. grated Parmesan cheese

2 tsp. parsley flakes
⅛ tsp. garlic powder
¼ tsp. salt
Dash of pepper
Paprika, optional

Remove stems from mushrooms; chop. In medium skillet, saute stems in margarine about 3 minutes or until tender. Remove from heat. Stir in bread crumbs, cheese, parsley flakes, garlic powder, salt and pepper. Use mixture to stuff mushroom caps. Place mushrooms (filled side up) on well-greased baking sheets. If desired, sprinkle tops with paprika. Bake at 350° for 15 to 20 minutes or broil for 5 to 8 minutes, until golden brown. Serve hot.

CORNISH HENS WITH ORANGE STUFFING

1 orange
¼ C. sliced green onion
¼ C. chopped celery
1 T. cooking oil
1 T. honey

½ of a 6 oz. pkg. (1½ C.)
  seasoned stuffing mix
2-1 to 1½ lbs. Cornish game hens,
  thawed and split lengthwise

Finely shred ¼ teaspoon peel from orange. Remove; discard remaining peel. Section orange over a bowl, squeezing out juices. Halve sections and set aside. Add water to the juices to equal 3 tablespoons. Cook onion and celery in hot oil until tender but not brown. For stuffing, toss together the orange peel, orange sections, onion mixture and stuffing with enough juice mixture to moisten. In a 15x10x1" baking pan spoon stuffing into 4 mounds. To roast, rinse hens; pat dry with paper towels. Place hens, cavity side down, over stuffing. Cover loosely with foil. Roast in a 375° oven for 30 minutes. Uncover; roast 20 minutes more. Combine honey and 1 tablespoon water;
56

brush over hens. Roast, uncovered, 15 minutes more or until hens are tender. Use spatula to transfer hens and stuffing to dinner plates.

NOTE: Use homemade bread dressing recipe if you are restricting salt.

HARVEST BEANS

2 C. frozen cut green beans or
  cut fresh green beans
¼ C. water
3 T. sliced green onions

½ tsp. chicken flavor instant
  bouillon
⅛ to ¼ tsp. cinnamon
Dash pepper
2 T. catsup

In medium saucepan, combine all ingredients except catsup. Bring to a boil; reduce heat. Simmer uncovered 8 to 10 minutes or until beans are tender. Stir in catsup. Serves 4 (½ cup each).
MICROWAVE: In 1-quart microwave-safe bowl or dish, combine beans, 3 tablespoons water and remaining ingredients except catsup; cover. Microwave on high for 9 to 12 minutes or until beans are tender. Stir in catsup.

APPLE SWEET POTATO SCALLOP

6 apples, peeled and sliced
6 sweet potatoes, peeled and
  sliced
1 C. fresh orange juice

Grated zest of 1 orange
1 tsp. cinnamon
1 C. crushed unsweetened corn
  flakes

Spray a 9x13x2" baking dish with nonstick spray. Place alternate layers of sweet potatoes and apples in baking dish, ending with apples. Pour orange juice mixed with zest over potatoes and apples and sprinkle with cinnamon. Bake, covered with foil, in a preheated 375° oven for 40 minutes. Remove foil and top with crushed cereal or bread crumbs. Bake 15 to 20 minutes more, until crumbs are lightly browned.

ORANGE-CRANBERRY SALAD

1 med. orange
1½ C. raw cranberries
1 (4-serving size) pkg.
  sugar-free gelatin (red or
  orange flavor)

¾ C. boiling water
½ C. cold water
Ice cubes

Quarter the orange and remove any seeds and half of the rind. Combine remaining orange and rind and the cranberries in food processor or food grinder and chop finely. Dissolve gelatin in boiling water. Combine cold water and ice cubes to make 1¼ cups. Add to gelatin and stir until slightly thickened; remove any unmelted ice. Add fruit mixture. Pour into 8" square pan or bowl and chill until set, about 2 hours. Spoon onto salad greens. Makes 6 servings.

BRAN-CRAN BREAD

2 C. whole cranberries
1½ C. oat-bran cereal
1 tsp. grated orange peel
¾ C. granulated sugar
⅓ C. brown sugar
½ C. chopped walnuts

2½ C. all-purpose flour
3 tsp. baking powder
½ tsp. ground allspice
¼ C. vegetable oil
1 container egg substitute

Chop the cranberries and add to the oat-bran cereal along with the orange peel and sugars. Mix together the flour, baking powder and allspice. Add the oil and egg substitute. Blend in the cranberry mixture and walnuts. Spray three 6x3" loaf pans with vegetable oil cooking spray and divide the batter between the pans. Bake for 40 to 50 minutes at 350° or until a toothpick comes out clean.

PUMPKIN-YOGURT PIE

½ loaf raisin Essene bread*
 (available in frozen food
 section of most health
 food stores)
1 C. canned pumpkin
⅓ C. frozen unsweetened
 apple juice concentrate
1 tsp. cinnamon

¼ tsp. ginger
½ tsp. freshly ground nutmeg
1-4 oz. can non-fat evaporated milk,
 well chilled
8 oz. non-fat peach yogurt
1 tsp. pure vanilla extract

Crumble raisin bread in blender or food processor (using steel knife). Lightly spray a 9" glass pie plate with non-stick spray. Spread crumbs evenly over surface; press lightly with hand. Bake in a preheated 375° oven for 8 minutes. Blend pumpkin with apple juice concentrate, cinnamon, ginger and nutmeg in a saucepan. Cook for 6 minutes on medium heat. Cool. Beat evaporated milk on high until stiff. Add stiffly beaten milk, yogurt and vanilla to cooled pumpkin mixture and blend well. Spoon into baked crust and chill for 4 hours or overnight. Can be frozen for future use. If frozen, remove from freezer 30 minutes before serving.

CHILDREN'S BIRTHDAY
PARTY MENU:
(Bear Theme)

Beary Tasty Nachos
Beary Healthy Pizza
Fruit Cup Salad
Teddy Bear Cake
Sweet Bear's Vanilla Ice Cream
Rasp "Beary" Punch

64

BEARY TASTY NACHOS

5-8" flour tortillas
2 med. tomatoes, peeled,
  seeded and chopped
1-4 oz. can diced green chili
  peppers, drained

½ tsp. chili powder
Several dashes bottled hot
  pepper sauce
1 C. shredded lowfat mozzarella
  cheese (4 oz.)

Stack tortillas and cut the whole stack into 8 wedges to make 40 wedges total. Spread evenly in a single layer on 2 medium baking sheets. Bake in a 375° oven for 10 to 15 minutes or until wedges are dry and crisp. Meanwhile, combine tomatoes, chili peppers, chili powder and hot pepper sauce. Spoon the tomato mixture over wedges and top with cheese. Broil 1 baking sheet at a time, 4" to 5" from heat, about 1½ minutes or until the cheese is melted. Place on a serving platter. Serve nachos at once. Makes 8 (5 nachos each) servings.

BEARY HEALTHY PIZZA

½ loaf frozen whole grain
  bread loaf, thawed
1-6 oz. can tomato paste
3 T. chopped onion
2 zucchini, sliced in ¼" rounds
5 stalks fresh asparagus,
  sliced in ½" pieces

¾ tsp. oregano
¼ tsp. basil
6 fresh mushrooms, sliced
½ green pepper, cut in strips
¼ C. chopped fresh parsley
¼ C. grated Parmesan cheese

Roll out dough into a 12" circle on a lightly floured surface. Place dough in a 12" microwave-safe browning grill. Spread tomato paste over crust. Arrange onion, zucchini and asparagus atop. Sprinkle oregano and basil over vegetables. Add mushrooms, pepper and parsley. Top with ¼ cup grated Parmesan cheese. Cover. Microwave on high (100% power) for 13 to 15 minutes, rotating ½ turn every 4 minutes. Makes 8 servings.

FRUIT CUP SALAD

1-3 oz. pkg. lemon gelatin
1-6 oz. can frozen orange juice
1-11 oz. can mandarin oranges,
  undrained
1 can drained fruit cocktail

2 sliced bananas
2 red chopped apples with skin
Desired combination of fresh fruits
1 C. boiling water
1-20 oz. can chunk pineapple,
  undrained

Dissolve lemon jello in boiling water. Immediately add orange juice, pineapple and mandarin oranges. Chill until syrupy. Add fruit cocktail, sliced bananas and chopped apples and any desired combination of fresh fruits (golden delicious apples, diced peaches in season, red or black grapes for color, cantaloupe). The orange juice keeps fresh fruit from discoloring. Keeps well for a week in the refrigerator.

TEDDY BEAR CAKE

3 C. all-purpose flour
2 C. granulated sugar
⅓ C. cocoa
2 tsp. baking soda
1 tsp. salt
2 C. water
¾ C. safflower oil
1 T. vinegar
2 tsp. vanilla
Flattened gumdrops

String licorice
Chocolate sprinkles
FROSTING:
⅔ C. sugar
½ C. water
1 T. corn syrup
3 egg whites
1 tsp. cream of tartar
⅓ C. sugar
1 tsp. vanilla

Preheat oven to 350°. Sift flour, sugar, cocoa, soda and salt into a 13x9x2" ungreased pan. In a medium bowl combine the water, oil, vinegar and vanilla. Pour into the flour mixture and blend well. Bake at 350° for 30 to 40 minutes or until wooden pick inserted in center comes out clean. Cool 10 minutes; carefully remove from pan and cool completely.   68

FROSTING: In a heavy saucepan, combine the sugar, water and corn syrup. Stir over low heat until sugar is dissolved. Raise the heat and cook without stirring until a few drops form a soft ball in cold water or until 238° on candy thermometer. Beat the egg whites with the cream of tartar until foamy. Slowly beat ⅓ cup sugar into egg whites to form soft peaks. Beating constantly at high speed, gradually pour the hot syrup over the beaten egg whites. Continue beating until frosting is completely cool and firm. Add vanilla. Cover a 15x11" heavy cardboard with foil. Center cake on foil-coated board. Frost sides and top of cake. Using a wax paper bear stencil traced from pattern, position 3 bear shapes on cake. Fill bear outlines with chocolate sprinkles if desired. Use string licorice and gumdrops to create balloon decorations. Makes 12 servings.

SWEET BEAR'S VANILLA ICE CREAM

2 C. skim milk
1 env. unflavored gelatin

1¼ C. sugar
2 C. skim evaporated milk
1½ tsp. vanilla

Heat skim milk to scalding point; do not boil. Remove from heat. Add gelatin and sugar. Mix until dissolved. Pour into blender. Whirl 3 to 5 minutes. Add evaporated milk; whirl 2 minutes. Chill 5 hours or overnight. Process in ice cream freezer according to manufacturer's directions. Stir in vanilla. Chill 30 to 60 minutes.

RASP "BEARY" PUNCH

1-10 oz. pkg. frozen raspberries
2 C. orange juice
2 C. lemonade

1-2 liter bottle of ginger ale
½ C. sugar
2 C. ice water
Ice cubes

Put frozen raspberries in punch bowl to thaw. Pour sugar over the raspberries and let set for an hour. Add the orange juice, lemonade and ice water. Mix well so sugar is dissolved and berries are all apart. Just before serving, add ginger ale and ice cubes.

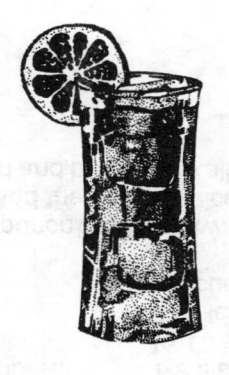

APPETIZERS

CHEESE-CARROT BALLS

¾ C. dry cottage cheese
2 T. buttermilk
½ C. grated carrots

⅛ tsp. salt
3 drops Tabasco
Minced parsley

Blend the buttermilk and cheese until smooth. Add carrots, salt and Tabasco. Chill for 30 minutes. Form mixture into balls and roll in parsley. Chill and pierce with cocktail picks. Makes 3 dozen.

CHICKEN ON STICKS

MARINADE:
2/3 C. soy sauce
1/4 C. sweet sherry
1 T. brown sugar

1/2 tsp. gingerroot
1 lg. clove garlic, minced
Juice of 1 lemon

1 lb. boneless, skinless
  chicken breasts in chunks

Pineapple chunks

Mix together the marinade ingredients. Add the chicken and marinate overnight in the refrigerator. Alternate chicken chunks and pineapple on chop sticks or bamboo picks. Broil for about 10 minutes until done.

74

CHILI CHEESE PIE

1-4 oz. can chopped green
  chilies
1 lb. grated lowfat mozzarella
  cheese

¾ lb. grated lowfat Cheddar cheese
1 C. egg substitute, slightly beaten

Arrange green chilies in a 9" pie plate and top with cheeses. Drizzle with egg substitute. Bake at 425° for 35 to 40 minutes. Remove from oven and let set for 10 to 15 minutes. Serve while warm and cut into squares.

CHUTNEY-CURRY DIP

1 C. low-cal mayonnaise	1 T. chutney
4 T. curry powder	Dash of Tabasco sauce
3 T. lemon juice	

Mix all ingredients thoroughly in blender. Excellent with fruit sticks and wedges and may also be used as dressing on fruit salad.

COCKTAIL MEATBALLS

Prepare your favorite meat loaf recipe; form (with a teaspoon) into small balls. Arrange the meatballs in a shallow baking dish. Microwave, uncovered, on high for 5 minutes, turning halfway through. Drain well. Combine the following:

1-12 oz. jar chili sauce   1-10 oz. jar grape jelly

Pour this sauce over the meatballs and microwave on high (100% power) for 10 minutes, stirring occasionally.

CRAB STUFFED MUSHROOMS

1 lb. lg. fresh mushrooms
½ C. oil & vinegar dressing
1 bunch fresh spinach
½ C. low-calorie mayonnaise

1½ T. grated onion
1 T. lemon juice
6 oz. crabmeat
½ C. grated lowfat Cheddar cheese

Marinate cleaned and stemmed mushrooms in oil and vinegar dressing for 1 hour. Drain. Wash spinach leaves and cook, covered, in heavy skillet until wilted. Drain; squeeze out excess moisture and chop. Blend mayonnaise, onion and lemon juice. Toss with crab and spinach. Stuff mushrooms; sprinkle with cheese. Bake at 375° for 15 minutes.

CRANBERRY-ORANGE DIP FOR FRUIT

1-8 oz. carton lemon or
  orange lowfat yogurt
½ C. cranberry-orange relish
¼ tsp. ground nutmeg
¼ tsp. ground ginger
1 med. apple
1 med. nectarine

Lemon juice
1 C. seedless grapes
1 C. strawberries
1 C. fresh pineapple, cut into chunks
  OR 1-8 oz. can pineapple chunks
  in juice, drained

Combine yogurt, relish, nutmeg and ginger. Cover and chill. Just before serving, core apple and remove pit from nectarine. Slice apple and nectarine; brush with lemon juice. Serve dip with apple and nectarine slices, grapes, berries and pineapple. Serves 10.

DILL DIP

MIX TOGETHER (liquefy
 in blender):

2 C. lowcal cottage cheese	½ C. fresh parsley, chopped
3 T. dill weed, crushed	½ C. fresh chives, chopped

Slice raw vegetables such as cucumbers, carrots, celery, green pepper, mushrooms and cauliflower to complement this diet-type appetizer.

GREAT POTATO SKINS

3 to 4 med. potatoes, baked
  and cooled
½ C. chopped onion
½ C. green pepper, chopped
¼ C. melted oleo

½ tsp. dill weed
½ tsp. salt
Dash of Tabasco sauce
1 C. shredded lowfat Cheddar
  cheese

Preheat oven to 450°. Cut potatoes lengthwise into wedges. Hollow out, leaving ¼" potato on skin. Cook onion and green pepper in oleo until tender. Add dill weed, salt and sauce. Spread on potatoes. Bake for 12 minutes or until crisp. Top with cheese. Heat to melt.

HAM-CHICKEN PINWHEELS

2 whole lg. chicken breasts,
  about 2 lbs. total, skinned
  and boned
1/8 tsp. dried basil, crushed
1/8 tsp. salt
Dash of pepper
Dash of garlic salt
4 thin slices fully cooked ham,
  about 3 oz.
2 tsp. lemon juice
Paprika

Rinse chicken and pat dry. Place 1 whole chicken breast between 2 pieces of clear plastic wrap; pound to 1/4" thickness. Repeat with the remaining chicken breast. Stir together the basil, salt, pepper and garlic salt; sprinkle on chicken. Cover each chicken breast with half of the ham; roll up from long side. Drizzle chicken with lemon juice; sprinkle with paprika. Bake in a 350° oven for about 30 minutes or until tender. Cover and chill; cut into 1/2" thick slices. If desired, serve chicken slices atop party bread or crackers. Makes 24 (1-slice each) servings.

LOW CAL VEGETABLE DIP

1 C. lowfat cottage cheese
¼ C. lowfat plain yogurt
½ tsp. fresh lemon juice

½ pkg. dehydrated vegetable
soup mix

Place all ingredients in a blender container. Cover and blend until smooth.
Serve with fresh vegetables. Makes 1 cup.

LOWFAT COTTAGE CHEESE DIP

1-12 oz. carton lowfat cottage
  cheese

1 T. fresh chives, chopped
½ tsp. hot pepper sauce

Blend well and serve. Makes 1½ cups.

LOWFAT CURRY DIP

1 C. plain yogurt   1 T. curry powder

Mix well and serve.

MARINATED BEEF

¼ C. finely chopped fresh
  green pepper
¼ C. finely chopped onion
1 C. of your favorite French
  or Italian dressing

4 C. cold, cubed, roasted or boiled
  beef (making certain all visible fat
  is removed from beef)

Combine all ingredients and marinate for 8 to 24 hours. Drain excess dressing before serving.

MEXICAN BEAN DIP

1-15 oz. can chili beans
1 clove garlic
½ C. nonfat yogurt
½ C. tomato sauce
½ sm. red onion, quartered
3 T. green chili salsa, or to taste

1 whole red or green pepper
  for serving
2 T. chopped tomato for garnish
1 T. chopped fresh cilantro for
  garnish

Place beans, garlic, yogurt and tomato sauce in blender or food processor.
Blend until smooth. Add onion and blend until chopped. Add salsa to taste
and blend briefly. Chill for several hours before serving to let flavors blend.

OATMEAL CRACKERS

1 C. ground oatmeal
6 T. all-purpose flour
½ tsp. baking powder
¼ tsp. salt

2 T. margarine, melted
6 to 8 T. boiling water
1 T. vegetable oil

Blend oatmeal, flour, baking powder and salt in bowl. Stir in melted margarine, then just enough boiling water to form ball. Roll dough out on a lightly floured board to 1/16" thickness. Cut out 2" rounds with 2" biscuit cutter. Heat large skillet over medium-high heat. Lightly brush with oil. Cook for 1 to 2 minutes per side or until lightly browned. Cool crackers on wire rack.

ONION DIP

1⅓ C. drained cottage cheese	2 T. lemon juice
½ C. water	3 T. dry onion soup mix
2 T. instant dry milk	

Blend cottage cheese, water, lemon juice, soup mix and instant dry milk.

PAPRIKA DIP

1 lb. farmer's cheese
2 T. grated onion
½ tsp. garlic powder

1 T. paprika
2 to 3 T. evaporated skim milk

Mix all ingredients in a blender and mix lightly or mix well with a spoon. If you want a firmer texture, mix with a spoon. Chill 24 hours before serving with Ry-Krisp or melba toast.

PICKLED GARDEN RELISH

½ head cauliflower
1 C. julienne fresh carrots
1 C. celery, cut into 1" pieces
¾ C. julienne fresh green
  peppers
4 oz. drained pimientos, cut
  into 1" pieces
3 oz. drained, pitted green
  olives

¾ C. wine vinegar
½ C. vegetable oil
2 T. sugar
¾ tsp. salt
½ tsp. ground oregano
¼ C. water

Cut cauliflower into flowerets, then cut each floweret into slices about ¼" thick. Mix ingredients in a large heavy frying pan and simmer, covered, for 5 minutes. Cool and refrigerate for 24 hours. Drain well and serve well chilled.

POTATO PUFFS

2 T. margarine, melted	1¼ C. all-purpose flour
1½ C. mashed boiled potatoes	1 T. sugar
⅓ C. finely chopped onion	⅓ C. margarine
⅛ tsp. ground black pepper	¼ C. egg substitute

In medium bowl, combine melted margarine, potatoes, onion and pepper; set aside. In medium bowl, combine flour and sugar; cut in ⅓ cup margarine until mixture resembles coarse crumbs. Stir in egg substitute until mixture is moistened. Knead dough on a lightly floured board until smooth, about 3 minutes. Roll dough to a 21x9" rectangle. Cut rectangle into three 21x3" strips. Place ½ cup potato filling, ½" high and ½" wide, down center of each strip. Fold 1 side of dough over filling, then roll strip over the remaining edge of dough. Seal seam well. Cut each roll into 14 pieces. Place on baking sheets, seam-side down; flatten slightly with palm of hand. Bake at 350° for 30 minutes. If desired, lightly brush with additional egg substitute. Broil for 2 to 3 minutes or until golden brown. Serve hot.

RADISH DIP

¾ C. finely chopped red
  radishes
½ of an 8 oz. pkg. Neufchatel
  cheese, softened
¼ C. plain lowfat yogurt

1 tsp. prepared horseradish
¼ tsp. dried dill weed
Dash of garlic powder
Assorted fresh vegetable dippers
  or crackers

In a small mixing bowl, stir together the radishes, Neufchatel cheese, yogurt, horseradish, dried dill weed and garlic powder. Cover and chill in the refrigerator at least 1 hour. Serve with fresh vegetables or crackers. Makes 10 (2 tablespoons each) servings.

RAISIN SPREAD

1 med. orange
¾ C. broken pecans
2 C. light raisins

½ C. reduced-calorie mayonnaise or
salad dressing
Orange slices, celery sticks or
assorted crackers

DO NOT peel the orange. Quarter and seed orange. In a food processor bowl process orange and nuts, covered, until finely chopped. Add half the raisins and all the mayonnaise. Cover, process until raisins are chopped. Add remaining raisins. Cover; process until finely chopped. Transfer nut spread to a covered container. Seal, label and freeze up to 3 months. Thaw in refrigerator several hours. To serve, spread on orange slices, celery sticks or crackers. Makes 40 (1 tablespoon each) servings.

RAW VEGETABLE DIP

½ C. low cal mayonnaise
½ C. low cal yogurt
1 T. fresh parsley, minced
⅛ tsp. garlic powder

1 tsp. chervil
1 tsp. thyme
1 tsp. rosemary leaves, crumbled

Combine all ingredients in a bowl. Chill before serving.

RUM WEINIES

1 pkg. turkey hot dogs   1 C. brown sugar
1 C. catsup   1 C. rum, light or dark

Combine catsup, brown sugar and rum in a baking dish. Cut 1 regular package turkey dogs into bite-sized pieces; stir into the sauce. Bake at 350° for 2 hours, stirring occasionally.

SALMON PATE

1 lb. can red salmon	½ tsp. onion powder
¾ C. (1½ sticks) margarine	½ tsp. paprika
1 tsp. lemon-pepper or	¼ tsp. monosodium glutamate
1 T. lemon juice and ¼	(MSG)
tsp. black pepper	

Drain salmon, removing bones and skin. Cream margarine until light and fluffy. Add salmon, lemon-pepper, paprika, onion powder and monosodium glutamate to creamed margarine and beat at medium speed until smooth. Scrape down bowl twice while combining margarine with other ingredients. Grease a 2-cup mold with softened margarine and press paté into mold. Chill for 3 hours. Unmold and garnish with olives or pimiento strips.

SCALLOPS

2 C. beer
½ tsp. salt
1 to 1½ tsp. finely ground
  pepper
40 scallops

Flour
2 T. olive oil
2 T. white vinegar

Combine beer, salt and pepper in medium bowl; add scallops and marinate for 15 minutes at room temperature. Drain scallops and coat with flour. Heat oil in large skillet and saute scallops until golden brown. Heat vinegar in small saucepan or ladle. Add to scallops and blend thoroughly. Makes 4 servings.

SEASONED SPINACH BALLS

1 pkg. frozen, chopped
  spinach
¼ C. margarine
½ C. egg substitute
1½ C. herb seasoned
  stuffing mix

½ C. shredded lowfat Cheddar
  cheese
2 C. grated Parmesan cheese
⅛ tsp. garlic powder

Defrost spinach. Beat egg substitute, add remaining ingredients. Add margarine last. Shape into 24 balls. Place in 8x12" baking dish. Bake covered, with wax paper, 5 to 7 minutes on high (100% power) in microwave or bake 12 to 15 minutes in regular oven at 350°.

SPINACH DIP

2 C. low calorie mayonnaise
½ C. parsley sprigs
½ sm. onion, cut up
1 sm. clove garlic
1 T. lemon juice

¼ tsp. pepper
1-10 oz. pkg. frozen, chopped
spinach, thawed and drained on
paper towels

In covered blender container blend all ingredients at high speed just until finely chopped. Cover and refrigerate at least 4 hours. Makes 2¾ cups. Can be made 1 or 2 days before serving.

STRAWBERRY-NUT NIBBLES

⅓ C. margarine
½ C. lowfat vanilla yogurt
1 C. all-purpose flour

¼ C. finely chopped pecans
⅔ C. low sugar strawberry spread

Cream margarine and yogurt with mixer. Stir in flour with mixer. Wrap dough in waxed paper and chill in freezer until firm (about 30 minutes). Roll half of dough out between two pieces of waxed paper; make into a 12" square. Cut each square into 16 squares. Combine pecans and strawberry spread in a bowl. Place 1 scant teaspoon of strawberry spread in center of each square. Pull corners of each square over strawberry spread, sealing edges. Bake at 350° for 15 minutes until slightly golden. Cool.

TUNA DIP

½ C. margarine
1-12 oz. can drained tuna fish
1 C. drained lowfat cottage
 cheese

1 T. lemon juice
¼ tsp. ground rosemary or garlic
 powder
¼ tsp. pepper

Cream margarine until light and fluffy. Add tuna, cottage cheese, lemon juice, rosemary and pepper. Beat at medium speed until smooth or mix in the blender. Chill at least 4 hours before serving.

TURKEY MEATBALLS WITH MUSTARD SAUCE

1 lb. ground raw turkey
⅓ C. cracker meal
¼ C. egg substitute
¼ C. chopped onion
2¼ tsp. dry mustard

½ tsp. tarragon leaves
1 C. unsweetened pineapple
  juice
2 T. honey
1 T. cornstarch

In medium bowl, thoroughly mix turkey, cracker meal, egg substitute, onion, ¼ teaspoon dry mustard and tarragon. Shape into 28 (1¼" each) balls. Place on a greased rack on a 15½x10½x1" baking pan. Bake at 375° for 30 minutes. Serve immediately. In small saucepan, over medium-high heat, stir together remaining dry mustard and remaining ingredients until mixture thickens and boils. Serve as a dipping sauce with meatballs.

FOR MICROWAVE: Prepare as above. Arrange 14 meatballs in 9" micro-wave-proof pie plate. Microwave on high (100% power) for 5 minutes, turning after 3 minutes. Repeat with remaining meatballs. To make sauce, combine

104

remaining ingredients in 2-cup microwave-proof measuring cup. Microwave on high for 3 minutes, stirring after 1½ minutes.

VEGETABLE DIP

MIX THOROUGHLY:

1 C. low cal mayonnaise	4 tsp. soy sauce (low-sodium)
1 tsp. ginger	1 T. vinegar
2 T. onion, minced	

Make 1 day in advance for mixture of flavors. Serve with pieces of fresh cauliflower, rutabaga, carrots, celery, zucchini, etc.

ZUCCHINI-STUFFED MUSHROOMS

20 lg. fresh mushrooms
1 sm. zucchini, shredded,
  ¾ C.
⅓ C. grated Parmesan cheese

2 T. sliced green onion
1 T. water

Remove the stems from mushrooms. Reserve the mushroom caps. Chop mushroom stems. In a medium saucepan combine the mushroom stems, zucchini, green onion and water. Cook and stir over medium heat until vegetables are tender. Drain. Stir Parmesan cheese into vegetable mixture. Divide vegetable mixture among the mushroom caps. Place stuffed mushrooms in a 9x13x2" baking pan. Bake in a 375° oven for 8 to 10 minutes or until the mushroom caps are tender. Serve warm. Makes 10 (2 mushrooms each) servings.

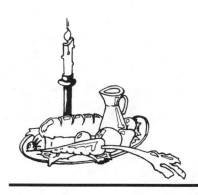

BREADS

CINNAMON APPLE MUFFINS

¼ C. brown sugar
2¼ C. oat-bran cereal
1¼ tsp. cinnamon
1 T. baking powder
¼ C. raisins
¼ C. chopped walnuts
2 T. vegetable oil

½ C. skim milk or evaporated
 skim milk
¾ C. frozen apple juice concentrate
2 egg whites
1 med. apple, cored and chopped

Mix dry ingredients in a large bowl. Combine the milk, apple juice concentrate, egg whites and oil in a blender or bowl. Add to the dry ingredients and mix. Add the chopped apples. Line the muffin pans with paper baking cups and fill. Bake at 425° for 17 minutes. Makes 12 muffins. These are delicious served with applesauce or spread with apple butter.

CRANBERRY COFFEE CAKE

1½ C. all-purpose flour
1 C. sugar
2 tsp. baking powder or
 low-sodium baking powder
2 tsp. grated lemon peel
Confectioners' sugar

½ C. unsalted margarine, softened
1-8 oz. container egg substitute
1 C. coarsely chopped cranberries

In a large bowl, with electric mixer at low speed, blend flour, sugar, baking powder, lemon peel, margarine and egg substitute. Beat at high speed for 4 minutes, scraping bowl occasionally; stir in cranberries. Spread into greased 13x9x2" baking pan. Bake at 350° for 40 to 45 minutes or until toothpick inserted in center comes out clean. Cool in pan on wire rack. Sprinkle with confectioners' sugar. Serve warm or cold.

DANISH PASTRY

1 pkg. yeast
¼ C. lukewarm water
6 T. sugar
¼ tsp. salt
1¼ C. scalded skim milk
1 C. margarine
½ C. egg substitute

1 tsp. vanilla extract
1 tsp. lemon juice
¼ tsp. mace
3½ C. sifted flour
1 egg white
¼ C. chopped walnuts

Place yeast in the water and stir until dissolved. Mix 3 tablespoons sugar, the salt, hot skim milk and ¼ cup margarine in bowl. Mix until margarine melts. Cool, then beat in the egg substitute. Beat in the yeast, vanilla, lemon juice, mace, and 3 cups flour. Knead lightly and form into a ball. Place in a fresh bowl, cover with a cloth and let rise in a warm place until double in bulk. Keep remaining margarine at room temperature. Punch down the dough and roll out on a lightly floured surface into a large square ¼" thick. Dot with half the margarine; fold dough over into thirds and press the edge together. Roll out again into a square and dot with the remaining margarine. Fold over, press edges together and chill for 15 minutes. Roll out and fold over. Repeat rolling and folding 3 times. Wrap the dough and chill for 30 minutes. Beat egg white until it starts to stiffen; mix in walnut and leftover sugar. Roll out the dough $1/3$" thick; cut into 2" squares. Spread lightly with walnut mixture; roll up diagonally and turn ends toward each other. Arrange on a baking sheet. Cover and let rise in a warm place for 30 minutes. Bake in a preheated 375° oven for 10 minutes or until browned. Makes 3 dozen.

LESS SWEET DINNER MUFFINS

1¼ C. oat-bran cereal
1 C. self-rising flour
1½ C. skim milk

2 egg whites
2 T. honey
3 T. vegetable oil

Blend the dry ingredients in a large bowl. Mix the milk and the remaining ingredients in a blender at low speed, then add to the dry ingredients and stir until just mixed. Bake at 425° for 15 minutes.

PANCAKES WITH YOGURT

1 C. egg substitute
2 C. plain non-fat yogurt
½ C. flour, sifted

¼ tsp. salt
1 tsp. baking soda

Beat egg substitute lightly and fold in yogurt. Blend dry ingredients; mix with eggs and yogurt using a wire whisk. Bake on a preheated griddle turning when top side is bubbly.

STREUSEL COFFEE CAKE

2 C. sifted flour
⅛ tsp. salt
2 tsp. baking powder
½ C. sugar
2 egg whites, beaten

½ C. orange juice
⅓ C. safflower oil
½ C. skim milk
1 T. grated orange rind

Sift the first 4 ingredients into a bowl. Make a well in the center and into it put the egg whites, orange juice, oil, milk and rind. Mix only until flour is moistened. Turn into an oiled 8" square pan. Prepare crumbs:

CRUMBS:
¼ C. sugar
¼ C. flour

2 T. corn oil margarine

Blend sugar and flour. Cut in the margarine until particles mix. Sprinkle over the top of the batter. Bake at 375° for 35 minutes or until browned. Cool on a rack.

ZUCCHINI PANCAKES
(MAKES 8-4" PANCAKES)

½ C. all-purpose flour
½ tsp. thyme leaves
¼ tsp. garlic powder
⅛ tsp. ground black pepper
3 C. shredded zucchini,
  about 2 med.

¾ C. egg substitute
⅓ C. chopped onion
2 T. margarine
Plain lowfat yogurt, optional

In small bowl, mix flour, thyme, garlic and pepper. In medium bowl, mix zucchini, egg substitute and onion. Stir in flour mixture. In large skillet, over medium-high heat, melt 1 tablespoon margarine. Drop zucchini mixture by ⅓ cupfuls into 4 mounds in skillet. Flatten each mound into a 4" pancake. Cook until golden brown on one side, about 2 to 3 minutes; turn and brown other side. Drain on paper towels; keep warm. Repeat to make 8 pancakes. Serve topped with yogurt, if desired.

118

MAIN DISHES

CHICKEN CURRY

3 lb. fryer, disjointed
¼ tsp. salt
¼ tsp. freshly ground
  black pepper
3 T. special oil
1 C. thinly sliced onions

1 T. curry powder
1 C. boiling water
1 T. cornstarch
½ C. skim milk
2 T. sesame seeds

Season the chicken with the salt and pepper. Heat the oil in a casserole, brown the chicken and onions in it. Sprinkle with the curry powder and add ½ cup water. Cover and cook over low heat 15 minutes. Add remaining water; recover and cook 15 minutes longer. Mix together the cornstarch and skim milk; stir into the gravy with the sesame seeds. Cook 15 minutes longer or until tender.

119

CHICKEN WITH CURRIED RICE

1 C. water
½ C. brown rice or long
  grain rice
2 T. thinly sliced green onion
½ tsp. curry powder
⅛ tsp. salt
⅛ tsp. ground ginger

2 tsp. margarine
1 C. sliced mushrooms
1 T. soy sauce
1 T. lemon juice
2 T. water
1 tsp. snipped parsley
1 whole med. chicken breast, about
  12 oz., skinned, boned, halved
  lengthwise

For Rice: In a small saucepan, combine water, rice, green onion, curry powder, salt and ginger. Bring to boiling, reduce heat. Cover and simmer brown rice 40 minutes or long grain rice 20 minutes or until liquid is absorbed. Meanwhile, pound chicken breast halves to flatten slightly. In a skillet cook the mushrooms over medium-high heat in margarine until just tender.

120

Remove with slotted spoon, reserving drippings in skillet. Add chicken and cook over medium heat for 8 to 10 minutes or until no longer pink, turning once. Place rice on individual serving plates. Top with chicken and mushrooms. Keep warm. Add soy sauce, lemon juice and water to pan drippings. Heat through, scraping up browned bits. Pour over chicken, mushrooms and rice. Serves 2.

EGGPLANT SKILLET DINNER

1 lb. ground beef, lean	½ C. water
¼ C. chopped onion	¾ tsp. oregano
¼ C. chopped celery	¾ tsp. chili powder
1-8 oz. can tomato sauce	1 medium-size eggplant, sliced in ½" slices

Brown and drain the ground beef, onion and celery. Stir in tomato sauce, water, oregano and chili powder. Mix well. Arrange the eggplant on top of the beef mixture in the skillet. Season with salt and pepper. Top with small amount of lowfat grated cheese and sprinkle with paprika. Simmer for 15 to 20 minutes. Serve.

FRUITY STUFFED PORK CHOPS

4 pork rib chops (lean),
 cut to 1¼ to 1½" thick
¼ C. chopped dried apricots
¼ C. orange juice
¼ C. finely chopped onion

Salt, as desired
1 T. margarine
1 C. chopped peeled cooking apple
2 T. packed light brown sugar

Slice pocket in each chop by cutting into center of chop from rib side, parallel to rib and surface of chop. Combine apricots and orange juice; let stand while preparing remaining ingredients. Cook onion in butter or margarine until tender. Add apple and cook until tender. Add apricots with juice and brown sugar; stir. Cook until juice evaporates. Cool slightly. Fill pockets in chops with equal amounts of fruit mixture (about ¼ cup). Place chops on rack of broiler pan. Broil about 4" from heat source 12 to 14 minutes. Turn chops. Broil 10 to 12 minutes or until chops are done. Season with salt, as desired. Makes 4 servings.

LOWFAT MEATBALLS

½ C. chopped onion
1 slightly beaten egg white
1 C. skim milk
1½ C. soft bread crumbs
¼ C. finely snipped parsley
½ tsp. salt
Dash of ground nutmeg
Dash of ground ginger

Dash of pepper
1½ lbs. lean ground beef
1 T. margarine
1 T. cornstarch
1½ tsp. instant beef bouillon
 granules
1½ C. water

Cook onion in a small amount of boiling water, about 5 minutes or until tender, then drain. In a medium mixing bowl, combine egg white and milk. Stir in onion, crumbs, parsley, salt, nutmeg, ginger and pepper. Add beef and mix well. Chill. Shape mixture into 1" meatballs. Place meatballs on a rack in a 15x10x1" baking pan. Bake at 375° for 15 to 20 minutes or until done. Transfer the meatballs to paper towels to drain well. In a large skillet, melt margarine, then stir in cornstarch and bouillon granules. Add water all at once. Cook and stir until thickened and bubbly; cook and stir 2 minutes more. Return the meatballs to skillet and heat through. Keep warm; serve with toothpicks. Makes 20 (3 meatballs each) servings.

ONE POT ORIENTAL CHICKEN

1 T. margarine
¼ C. chopped onion
2 T. cornstarch
3 T. soy sauce
⅔ C. chicken broth
1 T. brown sugar
¼ tsp. ground ginger
⅛ tsp. garlic powder
1½ C. cut up cooked
   chicken or turkey

1-16 oz. can cut green beans,
   drained and reserve liquid
1-16 oz. can sliced carrots, drained
   and reserve liquid
1-2½ oz. jar sliced mushrooms,
   drained (optional)
1 T. diced pimento, optional
Hot cooked rice
Chow mein noodles, optional

Melt margarine in 3-quart saucepan over medium heat. Cook onion until tender. Combine cornstarch and soy sauce. Stir cornstarch mixture, chicken broth, ⅔ cup reserved liquid, brown sugar, ground ginger and garlic powder into saucepan. Heat to boiling, stirring constantly. Boil and stir for 1 minute.

Add chicken, drained vegetables and pimento. Heat through. Salt and pepper to taste. Serve with hot cooked rice and chow mein noodles. Garnish with toasted sliced almonds, if desired.

ORANGE RUFFIE WITH PINEAPPLE

1½ lbs. orange ruffie fish
  fillets or snappers
Salt, to taste
1 onion
2 T. special oil
1 T. brown sugar

2 T. cornstarch
¼ C. vinegar or lemon juice
1 tsp. ground ginger
1 T. low-salt soy sauce
1 C. pineapple pieces and juice

Cut fish into serving-sized pieces and rub with salt. Place in 2- to 3- quart casserole. Peel and slice onion and saute in hot oil in pan. Mix all other ingredients and pour into pan, stirring until mixture thickens. Pour sauce over fish in casserole. Cover and bake at 350° for about 30 minutes. Serve with rice.

PEA AND PEPPER RISOTTO

¼ C. finely chopped onion
2 T. margarine
¾ C. long grain rice
¼ C. dry white wine
¼ tsp. dried thyme, crushed
⅛ tsp. ground black pepper
2 C. chicken broth

1 C. loose-pack frozen peas,
  packed
½ C. chopped red sweet pepper
⅓ C. shredded Parmesan cheese
Shredded Parmesan cheese,
  optional

In a 2-quart saucepan cook onion in hot margarine until tender but not brown. Add rice; cook and stir over medium-high heat until rice is light brown. Add wine, thyme and black pepper; cook and stir for 2 minutes. Add broth. Bring to boiling; reduce heat. Simmer, covered, 15 minutes. Add peas and sweet pepper. Cook and stir until heated through. Remove from heat; stir in the ⅓ cup cheese. Top with additional cheese. Makes 4 side-dish servings.

PORK WITH RHUBARB SAUCE

1-3 lb. lean pork loin center
  rib roast, about 8 ribs
½ tsp. salt
¼ tsp. coarsely ground pepper
½ lb. rhubarb, chopped, 2 C.

¼ C. frozen apple juice
  concentrate, thawed
2 T. honey
Several dashes of ground nutmeg
2 T. water
1 tsp. cornstarch

Season roast and place bone side down in a small shallow roasting pan. Insert a meat thermometer in the thickest part of the roast. Roast the pork, uncovered, in a 325° oven for 1¼ to 1½ hours or until thermometer registers 150°. Stir together the rhubarb, apple juice concentrate, honey and nutmeg. Bring to boiling and reduce heat. Cover and simmer for 10 minutes or until rhubarb is very tender. Stir water into cornstarch; stir into the rhubarb mixture. Cook and stir until thickened and bubbly. Cook and stir sauce for 2 minutes more. When the meat thermometer registers 150°, spoon some of the sauce over roast. Continue roasting pork 30 to 45 minutes more or until the thermometer registers 170°. Let roast stand 15 minutes before carving.

SALMON SQUARES WITH MUSHROOM PEA SAUCE

2 C. cooked rice (¾ C. uncooked)
½ C. egg substitute
2 C. (16 oz.) small curd cottage cheese (lowfat)
1 can (1 lb.) salmon, drained and flaked (may substitute ground ham, chicken or ground beef)
1 sm. onion, finely chopped
¼ C. green pepper, finely chopped
2 tsp. soy sauce (low-sodium)
1 C. soda cracker crumbs (low salt)

Combine all ingredients, except cracker crumbs. Spoon into a sprayed 12x7½x2" baking pan. Sprinkle cracker crumbs over top. Bake at 350° for 40 minutes or until firm in center. Cut into squares. Serve with mushroom pea sauce.

132

MUSHROOM PEA SAUCE:

3 T. margarine
1-4 oz. can sliced mushrooms, drained
3 T. flour
½ tsp. seasoned salt
1½ C. skim milk
1½ C. cooked peas, drained
2 T. pimiento, finely chopped

Cook mushrooms in margarine for 5 minutes. Stir in flour and salt. Gradually add milk. Cook until smooth and thickened, stirring constantly. Stir in peas and pimiento, cooking until hot. Spoon over salmon squares.

SOUFFLE WITH TUNA

2 T. margarine
1 C. sliced mushrooms
¼ C. chopped onion
2 T. all-purpose flour
1 C. skim milk
½ tsp. dill weed

1-3¼ oz. can low-sodium water-
  packed tuna, drained and flaked
⅛ tsp. ground black pepper
1-8 oz. container egg substitute

In medium saucepan, over medium-high heat, melt margarine. Add mushrooms and onion; cook, stirring occasionally for 2 to 3 minutes. Blend in flour; gradually add skim milk, stirring constantly until mixture thickens and boils. Remove from heat; stir in tuna, dill and pepper. In medium bowl, with electric mixer at high speed, beat egg substitute for 3 minutes. Gently fold into tuna mixture. Pour into greased 1-quart casserole or souffle dish. Bake at 325° for 35 to 40 minutes. Serve at once. Serves 4.

SPINACH QUICHE

¾ C. egg substitute
1-10 oz. pkg. chopped
  spinach, drained
2 C. lowfat cottage cheese
¼ C. mozzarella cheese
3 T. shredded lowfat cheese

½ tsp. Dijon mustard
¼ tsp. instant onion
¼ tsp. dry mustard
¼ tsp. red pepper
⅛ tsp. salt

Mix ingredients well. Pour into greased 9" pie plate. Bake at 350° for 35 to
40 minutes.

STIR-FRIED PORK AND PEA PODS

½ lb. lean, boneless pork,
  cut in thin strips
1 T. soy sauce
2 T. sherry
½ tsp. sugar
2 tsp. peanut oil or vegetable
  oil
¼ C. vegetable broth or
  chicken broth, canned
  broth or water

½ lb. fresh edible pea pods or
  1-10 oz. pkg. frozen pea pods
1 C. mung bean sprouts, rinsed
  drained, blotted dry
½ C. pimento strips
2 C. hot cooked rice
Additional soy sauce, if desired

Place pork strips in a long, shallow dish; sprinkle with 1 tablespoon soy sauce, sherry and sugar. Cover and refrigerate 30 minutes. Remove strips from marinade, reserving marinade; blot dry with paper towels. Place wok over high heat; add oil. When hot, add marinated pork; stir-fry until lightly browned. Pour in broth or water. Reduce heat to medium-low; cover and simmer 20 minutes. Then stir-fry until liquid evaporates. Stir in reserved marinade and pea pods; stir-fry 2 minutes. Stir in bean sprouts and pimento; stir-fry 1 minute. Serve over hot cooked rice with additional soy sauce, if desired. Makes 4 servings.

TUNA SOUFFLE

2 T. unsalted margarine
1 C. sliced mushrooms
¼ C. chopped onion
2 T. all-purpose flour
1 C. skim milk

1-3¼ oz. can low-sodium
  water-packed tuna, drained
  and flaked
½ tsp. dill weed
⅛ tsp. ground black pepper
1-8 oz. carton egg substitute

In medium saucepan, over medium-high heat, melt margarine. Add mushrooms and onion; cook, stirring occasionally for 2 minutes. Mix in flour and gradually add skim milk, stirring constantly until mixture thickens and boils. Remove from heat and stir in tuna, dill and pepper. In bowl with electric mixer at high speed, beat egg substitute for 3 minutes. Gently fold in tuna mixture. Pour into greased 1-quart casserole or souffle dish. Bake at 325° for 35 to 40 minutes or until puffed and golden. Serve immediately.

138

TURKEY JAPANESE CASSEROLE

1 lb. ground turkey
1½ C. long cooking rice
1 lb. mixed Japanese blend
  vegetables
1 to 2 C. shredded lowfat
  Cheddar cheese

1 can pinto beans without sugar
½ tsp. seasoning salt
Salt and pepper to taste

Brown turkey. Cook rice. When about done, add vegetables. Drain liquid from mixture. Mix ingredients in 9x13" pan. Top with cheese. Pop in microwave for 60 to 90 seconds or until cheese melts.

VEGETARIAN LASAGNA

1 lg. onion, chopped
3 cloves garlic, minced
1 lb. unpeeled eggplant,
 diced
2 zucchini, diced
¼ lb. fresh mushrooms, sliced
¼ C. salt-free tomato juice
1-28 oz. can plum tomatoes
 in puree
½ C. dry red wine
2 carrots, shredded
2 tsp. dried oregano, crushed
 or 4 tsp. fresh oregano
¼ C. minced fresh parsley
1 tsp. dried basil, crushed
 or 2 tsp. fresh basil
Freshly ground pepper
9 whole wheat lasagna noodles
1 lb. hoop cheese or skim milk
 ricotta
2 egg whites
¼ C. chopped fresh parsley
3 T. grated Sap Sago cheese,
 toasted

Cook onion, garlic, eggplant, zucchini and mushrooms for 15 minutes in tomato juice. Add tomatoes, wine, carrots, parsley, oregano, basil and ground pepper. Bring to a boil and simmer for 30 minutes, stirring occasionally. Cook, rinse and drain lasagna noodles according to manufacturer's directions. Process hoop cheese in blender or food processor until creamy. Add egg whites and chopped parsley and process briefly. Spray a 9x13" baking dish with nonstick spray. Spread a layer of vegetable sauce in dish, lay 3 strips of lasagna noodles lengthwise over sauce and place 4 dollops of hoop cheese on each noodle. Proceed with a second layer of sauce, noodles and hoop cheese, and a third layer of the same, ending with sauce. Sprinkle with Sap Sago cheese. Place dish on a baking sheet to catch those bothersome drips and bake in a preheated 350° oven for 45 minutes. Let stand 10 minutes before serving so that lasagna holds its shape.

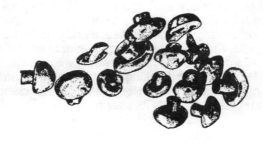

VEGETABLES

ARTICHOKES

3 fresh artichokes
3 T. chopped onion
3 cloves garlic
1½ C. dry white wine

2 T. olive oil
¼ C. safflower oil
Dash of salt
⅛ tsp. pepper
1 sliced lemon

Cut 1" off of top of artichoke; cut off stem and tips of leaves. Brush cut edges with lemon juice. Mix remaining ingredients. Bring to a boil. Place artichokes upright in mixture; cover and simmer until bottom leaves pull off easily. Drain. Serve hot or cold with homemade mayonnaise.

BROCCOLI AND DRESSING

3-10 oz. pkgs. frozen,
  chopped broccoli
6 T. margarine
4 T. flour
1 C. chicken broth

2 C. skim milk
⅔ C. water
2 C. herbed poultry stuffing
⅔ C. chopped walnuts

Cook broccoli until tender. Drain and pour into an oiled casserole. Melt 2 tablespoons margarine, stir in the flour, cook briefly and add the milk and chicken broth. Cook until thickened, stirring constantly. Set aside. Melt the remaining 4 tablespoons margarine in the ⅔ cup water. Mix with the herb dressing and walnuts. Pour the chicken broth over the broccoli, sprinkle with walnut mixture and bake at 400° for 20 minutes.

CHINESE STYLE CABBAGE

1 T. oil
3 C. finely shredded cabbage
1 C. celery, chopped
1 green pepper, chopped

1 onion, chopped
½ tsp. salt or less
⅛ tsp. pepper

Heat oil in skillet. Drop in vegetables and stir well. Cover tightly and steam for 5 minutes, stirring several times. Season with salt and pepper. Serve immediately. May top with soy sauce (low-sodium).

MARINATED VEGETABLES USING DIJON MARINADE

4 T. Dijon mustard
3 T. red wine vinegar
1 T. white wine vinegar
¼ tsp. salt
1 to 2 cloves garlic

½ tsp. basil
⅛ tsp. black pepper
2 drops hot sauce
12 T. safflower oil (¾ C.)
1 T. grated onion

Combine mustard and vinegar in blender. Add garlic, salt, black pepper, basil, onion and hot sauce; blend. While blending, add oil, 1 tablespoon at a time. Chill. Yield: 1¼ cups. Keeps for several weeks. Suggested vegetables to marinate are: carrot slices, mushrooms, zucchini slices, baby corn ears, cherry tomatoes, celery chunks, cauliflower, broccoli flowerets and cucumber sticks. Add vegetables to the marinade, refrigerate for several hours, drain vegetables thoroughly before serving.

STUFFED PEPPERS

2 med. green peppers
2 fresh tomatoes, peeled
 and chopped
¼ C. chopped onion
¼ C. chopped fresh
 mushrooms

2 T. chopped chives
⅛ tsp. basil
¼ tsp. pepper
½ C. bread crumbs
2 T. margarine, melted

Cut peppers in half lengthwise, remove tops and seeds. Cover with water and parboil 5 minutes. Remove from water and place cut side up in shallow baking dish. Combine remaining ingredients except bread crumbs and margarine and mix well. Fill each pepper half with mixture. Mix bread crumbs with melted margarine and sprinkle over filled peppers. Pour ¼" of water into bottom of dish and bake in 350° oven for 25 to 30 minutes. Serves 4.

STUFFED POTATOES

Scrub and prick 6 medium-size potatoes. Bake in 400° oven about 45 minutes or until cooked through. Cut the potatoes lengthwise, scoop out insides and mash the potato pulp. Blend in a covered jar until smooth:

1 T. vegetable oil	⅓ C. skim milk powder
½ C. skim milk	Salt and pepper to taste

Heat and add to mashed potatoes. Thin with skim milk if necessary. Beat until light and fluffy. Refill shells. Sprinkle with bread crumbs, chopped parsley, wheat germ, dash of paprika, Butter Buds. Return to oven and brown slightly. Serves 12.

STUFFED TOMATO BAKE

6 tomatoes
2 T. special margarine
¼ C. minced onions
½ lb. mushrooms
1 clove garlic

2 T. minced parsley
¼ tsp. salt
¼ tsp. freshly ground black pepper
2 T. dry bread crumbs

Use peeled tomatoes. Slice a 1" piece off the stem ends, scoop out the pulp and set tomatoes upside down to drain. Melt the margarine in a skillet; saute the onions and mushrooms 5 minutes. Put in the parsley, salt, pepper and bread crumbs. Stuff the tomatoes. Rub a baking dish with the garlic; arrange the tomatoes in it. Bake in a 375° oven 20 minutes or until the tomatoes are tender.

TWICE-BAKED POTATOES

4 potatoes
¼ C. hot skim milk

½ C. grated lowfat Cheddar cheese
Paprika

Bake potatoes in their skins. Cut potatoes in half lengthwise; scoop out centers. Mash . Beat with hot milk. Fill skins and sprinkle with cheese. Top with paprika. Bake at 400° for 20 minutes.

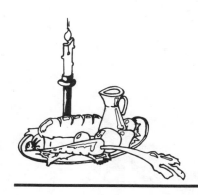

SALADS

AMBROSIA FRUIT SALAD

1-20 oz. can chunk pineapple
in juice or syrup
1-11 oz. can mandarin
orange segments
1½ C. seedless grapes

1 C. mini-marshmallows
½ C. nuts
¾ C. imitation sour cream
1 T. sugar

Drain pineapple and oranges. Combine remaining ingredients. Chill. Makes
4 to 6 servings.

CARIBBEAN PEACH SALAD

3 fresh peaches, sliced
2 bananas, peeled diagonally
 sliced into rounds
1 kiwi fruit, peeled, sliced
 into rounds
Lettuce leaves

2 rounds fresh pineapple, peeled
 cut into wedges OR 4 canned
 pineapple rings, halved
1 fresh strawberry, for garnish
Fresh Peach Dressing (recipe
 follows)

Reserve a quarter of one peach for dressing. Dip remaining peach slices and bananas in water with a little lemon juice. Arrange fruits on lettuce-lined plate. Pass Fresh Peach Dressing separately. Serves 4 to 6.

FRESH PEACH DRESSING: In blender combine the remaining ¼ peach, ¼ cup vegetable oil, 2 tablespoons orange juice, 2 tablespoons lime juice, 2 teaspoons grated fresh ginger. Blend until smooth. Makes about ⅔ cup.

152

CHEESE STUFFED TOMATO

Core the centers from 4 tomatoes. Turn upside down and allow to drain. Mix together 1 tablespoon skim milk, ¾ cup skim milk cottage cheese (or ¾ cup baker's cheese). Chop and add to the cheese 1 stalk celery, 2 to 3 green onions, ¼ green pepper, dash of salt and pepper to taste. Fill the tomatoes with the cheese, chill and serve on salad greens. Garnish the tomato with a sprig of parsley and a little paprika. Serves 4.

FENNEL-CHICKEN SALAD

⅓ C. olive oil or salad oil
¼ C. white wine vinegar
¼ tsp. fennel seed, crushed
¾ tsp. snipped fresh rosemary
  OR ¼ tsp. dried rosemary,
  crushed
¼ tsp. salt
Several drops bottled hot
  pepper sauce
2½ C. cubed cooked chicken
  or turkey

1½ C. sliced cauliflower or broccoli
  flowerets
3 med. plums, pitted and sliced OR
  1-8½ oz. can whole unpitted
  purple plums, drained, pitted
  and sliced
½ C. sliced radishes
4 C. shredded Chinese cabbage
¾ C. English walnuts

In a medium salad bowl combine oil, wine vinegar, fennel, rosemary, salt and hot pepper sauce. Add chicken or turkey, cauliflower or broccoli, plums and radishes. Toss lightly to coat. Cover and chill for 2 hours. To serve, stir mixture in bowl. Add the Chinese cabbage and nuts. Toss lightly to mix. Makes 6 servings.

FRUIT AND YOGURT DELIGHT

1 pkg. plain, unflavored gelatin
1 C. fresh grapefruit juice,
 heated to boiling
1 C. nonfat yogurt
3 C. grapefruit segments (about 3
 whole grapefruit, peeled,
 sectioned, and cut into 1" pieces)
1 C. orange segments (about 2
 navel oranges, peeled,
 sectioned, and cut into 1"
 pieces)

¾ C. seeded red grapes, halved
Curly endive or red or green leaf
 lettuce for serving
2 kiwi fruit, peeled and sliced for
 garnish
4 sm. sprays whole red grapes,
 for garnish

Dissolve gelatin in heated grapefruit juice. Add yogurt to gelatin mixture. Stir with a whisk until smooth. Chill until thick as unbeaten egg whites. Reserve 6 grapefruit segments and 4 orange segments for garnish. Fold drained, cut

156

grapefruit, orange and grapes into chilled yogurt mixture. Rinse a 1-quart mold with cold water and add fruit gelatin mixture. Cover with plastic wrap and chill until firm or overnight.

To Unmold and Serve: Unmold onto a platter lined with one of the suggested greens. Run a metal spatula around the edge of the mold to loosen, then invert mold over platter and shake gently. Garnish with orange and grapefruit segments, sliced kiwi and grape sprays.

MARINATED SCALLOP SALAD

8 oz. fresh or frozen scallops
⅓ C. orange juice
3 T. white wine vinegar
2 T. cooking oil
⅓ C. chopped red onion

1 T. parsley
2 tsp. canned chopped jalapeno
  chili peppers
2 C. shredded lettuce
1 sm. cucumber, thinly sliced
Lemon wedges

In a medium saucepan cook the scallops in boiling water for 1 minute or until scallops are opaque. Drain and rinse under cool water to stop cooking. Combine orange juice, white wine vinegar, cooking oil, onion, parsley and jalapeno peppers. Add to scallops; cover and chill at least 2 hours or up to 24 hours. To serve, line each serving plate with half the lettuce; arrange half of the cucumbers in circle atop lettuce. Spoon scallop mixture in center of each plate. Serve with lemon wedges. Makes 2 servings.

158

MINT JULEPEACH SALAD

2-3 oz. pkgs. lemon gelatin
1½ C. hot water
½ C. frozen lemonade
  concentrate
1-7 oz. bottle ginger ale,
  chilled
⅛ tsp. mint flavoring

2 C. fresh peach balls
1 C. honeydew melon balls
1 C. seedless green grapes,
  cut in halves

Dissolve gelatin in hot water. Add lemonade concentrate, ginger ale and mint flavoring. Stir to dissolve and chill until partially set. Fold in remaining ingredients. Turn into 1½-quart mold or 8 individual molds. Chill until firm.

ORIENTAL NOODLE SALAD

1 lb. fresh noodles, Chinese-
  style*
1-8 oz. container plain yogurt
2 T. soy sauce
4 green onions with tops,
  sliced diagonally

1½ tsp. Dijon-style mustard
Salt and pepper to taste
1 C. shredded carrot
6 oz. fresh, blanched snow peas
  OR 1-6 oz. pkg. frozen snow
  peas, thawed
1 to 2 T. toasted sesame seeds

Cook noodles in boiling water for 2 minutes, or until tender. Drain immediately and rinse under cold water until noodles are room temperature; drain. Combine yogurt, soy sauce, green onion, mustard, salt and pepper in large bowl. Add noodles and carrots, tossing to coat evenly. To serve, arrange noodle mixture on platter; top with snow peas. Sprinkle with sesame seeds. Makes 8 servings.

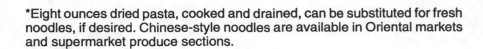

*Eight ounces dried pasta, cooked and drained, can be substituted for fresh noodles, if desired. Chinese-style noodles are available in Oriental markets and supermarket produce sections.

RING OF MELON SALAD

SALAD:
1 honeydew melon   1 pt. (2 C.) strawberries, sliced
Lettuce leaves
1 C. blueberries

MARSHMALLOW CREME DRESSING:
¾ C. marshmallow creme   ½ to 1 tsp. grated orange peel
2 T. orange juice

Cut honeydew crosswise into ¾" slices; remove seeds and rind. Cut decorative edge on 4 or 5 center rings, if desired; place on lettuce-lined salad plates. Cut remaining melon into cubes. Combine melon cubes, strawberries and blueberries; spoon into center of melon rings. Combine all dressing ingredients; spoon over fruit. Serves 4 to 5.

162

SALMON MOUSSE

1-16 oz. can red salmon,
drained, skinned and
bones removed
½ C. nonfat yogurt
¼ C. lowfat cottage cheese
(rinsed and drained)
1 T. lemon juice
½ tsp. dry horseradish
1 tsp. dry mustard or salt-
free Dijon mustard with
herbs
Few grains cayenne pepper

2 pkgs. plain, unflavored gelatin
1½ C. chicken stock
1 C. skimmed evaporated milk,
well chilled
3 C. finely shredded romaine
Red lettuce leaves for serving
6 limes or lemons for garnish
1-4 oz. jar chopped pimiento,
drained and chopped for garnish

Combine salmon, yogurt, cottage cheese, lemon juice, horseradish, mustard
and cayenne in blender or food processor. Blend until smooth. Do not over

164

mix. Soften gelatin in ½ cup of the cool chicken stock. Liquefy over hot water or heat and add to salmon with the remaining cup of chicken stock. Whip thoroughly chilled milk in chilled bowl until stiff. Fold salmon mixture and romaine into whipped milk. Spray a 6-cup fish mold with nonstick spray and fill. Chill until set. Serves 12.

STRAWBERRIES AND ASPARAGUS DAZZLERS

DRESSING:
¼ C. lemon juice
2 T. oil
2 T. honey

SALAD:
2 C. fresh asparagus spears,
  cut into 1" pieces
2 C. fresh strawberries, sliced

In jar with tight-fitting lid, combine all dressing ingredients; shake well. Partially cook asparagus in rapidly boiling water for 3 to 5 minutes or until crisp-tender; drain. Rinse with cold water. Arrange asparagus and strawberries on 4 individual salad plates. Drizzle with dressing. Serves 4.

166

TOFU AND GREENS

SALAD:
4 C. torn mixed salad greens
  (Chinese cabbage,
  spinach, endive)
1 C. cubed tofu
1 C. fresh bean sprouts
¼ C. sesame seeds

DRESSING:
¼ C. rice wine vinegar or white
  vinegar
2 T. sesame oil
1 T. soy sauce (low-sodium)
½ tsp. sugar

In a large bowl, combine greens, sprouts, tofu and sesame seeds. In jar with tight-fitting lid, combine all dressing ingredients and shake well. Just before serving, toss salad with dressing.

DESSERTS

BOYSENBERRY SORBET

1-16 oz. pkg. frozen
unsweetened boysenberries
or strawberries

3 T. frozen unsweetened apple juice
concentrate
⅔ C. nonfat yogurt
¼ C. instant nonfat dry milk

Place half the frozen berries in blender or food processor and puree. Add remaining fruit and frozen apple juice concentrate. Puree. Add yogurt and dry milk. Process until sorbet is formed. Pour into an 11x7" metal or glass baking pan. Freeze until nearly frozen solid. Return mixture to blender or food processor. Process until broken into small pieces; then process until creamy. Place mixture into individual dishes or hollowed lemon or orange shells or in one large container, cover with plastic wrap and return to freezer. To serve, remove from freezer about 15 minutes before serving.

COCOA MINT TOFU PIE

1½ lbs. tofu, soft or firm style
½ C. light honey
½ C. sifted cocoa powder
½ tsp. ground cinnamon

2 T. pure vanilla extract or 2 lg. fresh
minced mint leaves

Blend ingredients until very smooth. Pour into unbaked pie shell and bake at 425° for about 15 minutes. Sprinkle with nuts and return to oven until lightly browned.

DELICIOUS APPLE TORTE

5 to 6 apples, peeled, cored, chopped and marinated in 3 oz. unsweetened frozen orange juice and 1 T. dry sherry for 4 hours or overnight

1-6 oz. can frozen unsweetened apple juice concentrate

⅔ C. ripe bananas, mashed

½ C. muscat raisins, plumped 15 minutes in hot water to cover

1¼ C. whole wheat pastry flour
1¼ C. unbleached white flour
¼ C. soy flour
2 tsp. low-sodium baking powder
2 tsp. baking soda
2 tsp. cinnamon
⅛ tsp. freshly ground nutmeg
⅛ tsp. allspice
4 egg whites, stiffly beaten
1½ tsp. pure vanilla extract
1 C. Grape-Nuts

Combine apples, apple juice concentrate, raisins and bananas in a bowl. Sift dry ingredients into apple mixture. Stir until flour disappears and fold in stiffly beaten egg whites and vanilla. Pour into a nonstick bundt pan that has been sprinkled with Grape-Nuts and bake in a preheated 325° oven for 1½ hours. Cool and cover with plastic wrap; let stand several hours or overnight before serving. To serve: Place slices of torte on individaul plates and serve each with a dollop of whipped nonfat milk (recipe below).

WHIPPED TOPPING:
⅓ C. water   1 T. sugar
1 to 2 tsp. lemon juice   ¼ tsp. vanilla
⅓ C. skim milk powder

Blend water, lemon juice and skim milk powder. Chill for 1 to 2 hours in freezer. Chill all utensils in freezer also. Beat until stiff and add sugar and vanilla.

FROZEN APRICOT APPLE CREAM

6 whole dried apricots,
  coarsely chopped
½ C. unsweetened apple juice
½ C. lowfat plain yogurt

3 lg. or 4 med. golden delicious
  apples, peeled, cored and sliced
1 T. apricot or peach brandy

Combine the apricots, apple juice and apples in a 1½-quart micro-proof casserole. Cover tightly and microwave on high for 7 to 9 minutes or until apples are tender, stirring once. Pour mixture into bowl or food processor or blender. Add yogurt and brandy; process until mixture is smooth. Divide mixture between 8 individual (plastic or paper) dessert cups and freeze about 30 minutes; or freeze in 1-quart covered container. Soften at room temperature for 15 minutes or microwave on medium for 40 seconds before serving. Serves 8.

174

FROZEN BERRY YOGURT

1 pkg. unflavored gelatin
¼ C. water
2-8 oz. cartons plain lowfat
 yogurt
½ C. sugar
2 egg whites

2 C. chopped fresh or frozen
 unsweetened blueberries,
 strawberries or whole raspberries
1 tsp. vanilla
¼ C. sugar

In a small saucepan soften gelatin in the water for 5 minutes. Cook and stir over low heat until gelatin dissolves. Cool slightly. Stir together yogurt, berries, gelatin mixture, ½ cup sugar and vanilla. Turn mixture into an 11x7x1½" baking pan. Cover and freeze for 45 to 60 minutes or until partially frozen around the edges. In small mixer bowl beat egg whites until soft peaks form (tips curl over). Gradually add the ¼ cup sugar, beating until stiff peaks form (tips stand straight). Turn the frozen mixture into a large mixer bowl. Beat with an electric mixer until nearly smooth. Fold the egg whites into berry mixture. Return to pan. Cover and freeze for 4 to 6 hours or until firm. Scoop to serve. Makes 11 ½-cup servings.

LEMONY CHEESE PIE

1-16 oz. carton lowfat cottage
  cheese
5 egg whites
¾ C. evaporated skim milk
1 T. instant nonfat milk
⅔ C. frozen unsweetened
  apple juice concentrate
3 T. cornstarch
¼ C. fresh lemon juice

2 tsp. grated lemon zest
1 tsp. pure vanilla extract
¼ tsp. cream of tartar
1½ C. unsweetened wheat flakes
  with raisins
½ C. sliced almonds
1 C. sliced fresh strawberries

Process cheese, 2 of the egg whites and ¼ cup of the skim milk in food processor or blender until creamy and smooth. Add remaining milk, instant milk and apple juice concentrate and blend thoroughly. Add cornstarch, lemon juice, zest and vanilla extract and blend. Beat remaining 3 egg whites with cream of tartar until stiff, not dry (do not slide around bowl). Pour cheese

178

mixture over stiffly beaten egg whites and fold carefully. Spray an 8" pie plate or springform pan with nonstick spray and sprinkle wheat flakes and raisins over bottom of pan. Pour cheese mixture into pan and top with almonds. Place in a preheated 325° oven and bake 50 to 60 minutes, until firm and lightly browned. Turn off oven and let pie sit in oven 30 minutes. Finish cooling on a rack at room temperature. Chill before serving. To serve, cut pie in wedges and top with strawberries.

LEMON YOGURT PIE

CRUST:
⅓ C. margarine
1½ C. 100% Bran,
  finely rolled
¼ C. finely chopped walnuts
⅓ C. light brown sugar,
  firmly packed

FILLING:
8 oz. special whipped topping
  (see substitution chart)
2-8 oz. containers lemon yogurt,
  nonfat
1-8 oz. can crushed pineapple,
  drained
1 thin lemon slice

Preheat oven to 375°. In medium saucepan, over low heat, melt margarine; remove from heat and stir in 100% Bran crumbs, walnuts and brown sugar. Press evenly onto bottom and sides of 9" pie plate. Bake for 8 to 10 minutes; cool. In a large bowl, fold together whipped topping, lemon yogurt and pineapple; spoon into prepared crust. Freeze 5 hours or overnight until firm. Garnish with lemon slice.

MELON MIX WITH GINGER SAUCE

⅔ C. white grape juice
2 tsp. cornstarch
2 tsp. snipped crystallized
  ginger
2 T. dry sherry

½ med. cantaloupe, peeled
  and thinly sliced
2 C. casaba melon chunks
2 C. honeydew melon balls

In a medium saucepan combine grape juice, cornstarch and crystallized ginger. Cook and stir until thickened and bubbly. Cook and stir for 1 to 2 minutes more. Stir in sherry. To serve, arrange the melon slices, chunks and balls on individual dessert plates. Drizzle hot sauce over fruit. Makes 4 servings.

MELON MOUSSE

2 C. cubed honeydew,
  cantaloupe, Persian,
  casaba or crenshaw melon
2 T. melon or orange liqueur

1 env. unflavored gelatin
¼ C. water
⅓ C. frozen whipped dessert
  topping, thawed

Place cubed honeydew melon and melon liqueur in a blender container or food processor bowl. Cover and blend or process until smooth. In a medium saucepan stir together gelatin and water. Let stand 5 minutes. Cook and stir over low heat until gelatin is dissolved. Stir in pureed honeydew mixture. Chill to the consistency of corn syrup, stirring several times. When gelatin is partially set (consistency of unbeaten egg whites), fold in the dessert topping. Pour into 4 individual ½-cup molds. Chill about 2 hours or until firm. To serve, unmold onto serving plates. Garnish with fresh mint, if desired. Makes 4 servings.

PINEAPPLE SNOW ON STRAWBERRIES

1-4 serving size pkg. low
   calorie pineapple flavored
   gelatin
1¼ C. boiling water
Nonstick spray coating

2 egg whites
2 C. strawberries
1 T. sugar
1 T. cherry liqueur

Combine gelatin and boiling water; stir to dissolve. Cool. Spray bottoms of 8 clear plastic 9-ounce drink cups with nonstick coating. Wash and hull strawberries. Slice 2 or 3 strawberries to make eight ¼" thick slices. Dip the slices into the cooled gelatin mixture and place in the center of the bottom of drink cups.

For Sauce: Place remaining strawberries in blender container or food processor bowl. Add sugar and cherry liqueur. Cover and blend or process until strawberries are smooth. Cover; chill. Chill the gelatin in the refrigerator for 30 minutes or until the consistency of unbeaten egg whites. Remove from refrigerator. In a large mixer bowl combine gelatin mixture and egg whites. Beat with an electric mixer on high speed for 8 minutes or until soft peaks form (tips curl over). Spoon the mixture into the prepared cups, filling ⅔ full. Cover each cup with plastic wrap. Chill several hours or until firm. To serve, spoon sauce onto individual dessert plates. Unmold pineapple mixture in center of each plate. If desired, garnish each serving with a mint sprig. Makes 8 servings.

RASPBERRY ANGEL FOOD CAKE

10 egg whites, room temp.
1¼ tsp. cream of tartar
¼ tsp. salt
1 tsp. vanilla extract
½ tsp. almond extract

1¼ C. sugar
1 C. cake flour
1 C. fresh raspberries
Raspberry Amaretto Sauce
  (recipe follows)

Preheat oven to 325°. In a large bowl, beat egg whites, cream of tartar and salt with an electric mixer until they form soft peaks. Add vanilla and almond extracts and gradually add the sugar, beating until stiff and shiny. Sift the flour onto the shiny egg whites and sprinkle raspberries over the top. Gently fold in the flour and raspberries with a rubber spatula.Place mixture in a 10" ungreased tube pan and bake for 40 minutes or until an inserted toothpick comes out clean. Invert onto a cake rack. Cool completely, then invert onto a platter. Remove pan carefully (loosen around edges, if necessary) and serve with Raspberry Amaretto Sauce.

RASPBERRY AMARETTO SAUCE:

2 C. raspberries, fresh or frozen	1 T. lemon juice
½ C. confectioners' sugar	4 T. Amaretto liqueur

In a blender or food processor fitted with a steel blade, puree raspberries. Add sugar, lemon juice and Amaretto and continue to process until smooth. Strain to remove seeds. Serve with Raspberry Angel Food Cake.

RASPBERRY YOGURT MOUSSE

1½ C. unsweetened, frozen
  raspberries, thawed
¼ C. apricot nectar
1 env. unflavored gelatin
1½ C. vanilla lowfat yogurt

½ C. fresh raspberries, (optional)
  or use strawberries or blueberries
  or peaches
4 sprigs mint (optional)

Puree raspberries in blender. Place in medium-sized bowl and set aside. Pour nectar in small saucepan. Sprinkle gelatin mixture on top. Let stand for 1 to 2 minutes until softened. Over low heat, warm gelatin mixture just until dissolved. Using small whisk, gradually beat gelatin mixture into puree. Refrigerate for 10 to 15 minutes, or until consistency is like lightly beaten egg whites. Using hand-held electric mixer at low speed, beat mixture for about 30 seconds until fluffy. Transfer mousse to 3-cup mold or 4 individual serving dishes. Chill several hours until firm. Remove mousse from mold. Garnish with fresh fruit and mint.

188

SORBET AND FRESH FRUIT

PEACH SORBET:
1½ tsp. unflavored gelatin
½ C. water
2 C. frozen peach slices
  without syrup, partially thawed

⅓ C. peach schnapps
¼ C. sugar
3 T. lemon juice

RASPBERRY SORBET:
1½ tsp. unflavored gelatin
½ C. water
10 oz. pkg. frozen raspberries
  with syrup, partially thawed

⅓ C. raspberry-flavored liqueur
2 T. lemon juice
Papaya, kiwi fruit, fresh raspberries

In small saucepan, combine gelatin and water; let stand 1 minute. Stir over medium heat until gelatin dissolves; set aside. In food processor bowl with metal blade or blender container, place partially thawed fruit; process until

190

smooth. Add liqueur, sugar for peach sorbet, lemon juice and gelatin mixture; process until smooth. Pour sorbet into 9" square pan; cover. Freeze until almost firm, stirring occasionally, about 3 to 5 hours.

STRAWBERRY PIE DELUXE

1 qt. fresh strawberries or
  1-16 oz. pkg. frozen
  unsweetened whole
  strawberries
½ C. sugar

1 env. unflavored gelatin
1 T. lemon juice
1 baked 9" pastry shell
1 lg. banana

Thaw frozen strawberries, reserving juices. Using a potato masher, crush 3 cups strawberries. Halve or slice remaining berries and set aside. Strain crushed strawberries; add water to juice to equal 1 cup of liquid. Reserve crushed strawberries. In a medium saucepan stir together sugar and gelatin. Add the 1 cup liquid. Cook and stir over medium heat until gelatin and sugar are dissolved. Stir in reserved crushed strawberries and lemon juice. Transfer mixture to a mixing bowl. Chill until partially set (the consistency of unbeaten egg whites). Pour half of the mixture into cooled pastry shell. Thinly slice banana; arrange in a single layer over berry mixture. Top with remaining

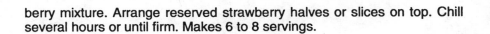

berry mixture. Arrange reserved strawberry halves or slices on top. Chill several hours or until firm. Makes 6 to 8 servings.

TOFU "ICE CREAM"

2 egg whites
8 oz. tofu
1 T. vanilla
1 tsp. Equal sweetener

2 C. unsweetened strawberries, frozen
4 T. tropical punch, sugar-free Kool-Aid plus ¼ C. water

In food processor or blender, whip egg whites until foamy. Add remaining ingredients. Should be thick and ready to eat.

NOTE: Strawberries should be frozen when added. This is what makes it thick and cold. Tofu is soy bean curd. A good source of protein with no cholesterol and very low in calories. This is very much like the soft serve frozen yogurt.

TUTTI FRUTTI ICE
A DAIQUIRI-LIKE FROZEN DESSERT

1-16 oz. pkg. frozen mixed
  fruit, unsweetened
½ C. water

½ of a 6 oz. can (⅓ C.) frozen
  lemonade concentrate
¼ C. rum

Thaw frozen mixed fruit. In a blender container or food processor bowl combine half of the mixed fruit, half of the water, half of the frozen lemonade concentrate and half of the rum. Cover and blend or process until smooth. Transfer mixture to a 9x5x3" loaf pan. Repeat with the remaining mixed fruit, water, frozen lemonade concentrate and rum. Cover loaf pan with foil; place in the freezer for 4 to 5 hours or until almost firm. Transfer the frozen fruit mixture to a chilled large mixer bowl. Beat with an electric mixer on medium speed about 2 minutes or until fluffy. Return the fruit mixture to the cold loaf pan. Cover and freeze fruit mixture about 6 hours more or until firm. Makes 8 servings.

INDEX

● ● ● ● ● ● ● ● ● ● ● ● ● ● ● ●

APPETIZERS

VEGETABLES